MYTHS AND MYSTERIES
OF NEW MEXICO

MYTHS AND MYSTERIES SERIES

MYTHS AND MYSTERIES OF NEW MEXICO

True stories
of the unsolved and unexplained

Barbara Marriott

Guilford, Connecticut

For Tyler, Casey, and Matt,

who introduced me to the mysteries of youth

and taught me a new kind of love

Copyright © 2011 by Morris Book Publishing, LLC

Layout: Kevin Mak
Project editor: Gregory Hyman
Map: M. A. Dubé © Morris Book Publishing, LLC

Library of Congress Cataloging-in-Publication Data is available on file.

ISBN 978-0-7627-5873-9

Printed in the United States of America

10 9 8 7 6 5 4 3 2 1

CONTENTS

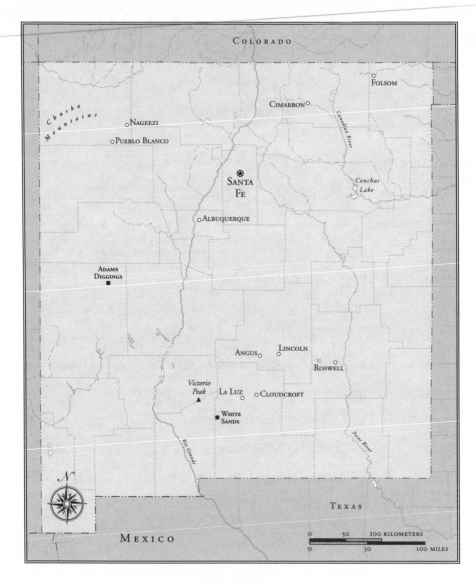

COLORADO

FOLSOM

Chuska Mountains

CIMARRON

Canadian River

NAGEEZI

PUEBLO BLANCO

Conchas Lake

SANTA FE

ALBUQUERQUE

ADAMS DIGGINGS

ANGUS   LINCOLN

ROSWELL

Victorio Peak   LA LUZ   CLOUDCROFT

WHITE SANDS

Pecos River

Rio Grande

N

TEXAS

MEXICO

0   50   100 KILOMETERS

0   50   100 MILES

NEW MEXICO

ACKNOWLEDGMENTS

The hardest thing to find is pictures of myths and mysteries. I did find pictures of people and places related to those mysteries, although that, too, was difficult. For pictures of Choco Canyon, I have to thank Bob Stuart. Terry Delonas gave me details and insight into the Noss family and the Victorio Treasure, and Bonnie McGuire sent me the pictures of Victorio Peak. James Owens provided the pictures of the Mayberry and Nelson graves. To Tricia Warwick, executive assistant for the New Mexico Public Regulation Commission, thank you for your help with the La Llorona myth.

Jeff Meldrum helped me find Sasquatch pictures, and Paul Harden generously supplied his Adams Diggings map. Thomas Carey was invaluable in helping me make sense of the Roswell incident.

And, of course, Mike—photographer, chauffeur, research assistant, and idea man—was indispensable. To all of them I owe my deepest thanks. Without their help, we would all be wondering about the myths and mysteries of New Mexico.

INTRODUCTION

B orn in the fury of fire, New Mexico is a mischievous child that has offered herself up in the most outlandish ways. Her lushness enticed ancient man to hunt her plentiful game, and she lured greedy old-timers with promises of riches, encouraged men to go beyond the bounds of science, and flirted with beings from outer space. Yet she has never been conquered and remains a mystery.

Part of her charm is her palette of colors and textures and the contrast of cultures and nature. From the black, jagged volcanic-rock formations; the smooth, glistening White Sands; the mountains and canyons dressed in somber or vivid hues; the ancient Native American cultures seeped in mystery; the obvious outlaws and pioneers . . . all this and more is New Mexico.

Nature may have conjured her up, but man contributed the greed and the legends.

Gold! That's what man wanted, and he found it in "The Treasure of Victorio Peak" and in "The Lost Adams Gold." Power, control, and riches are what man was after, and it led to "Lincoln: The Town of Legends." It also led to murder and questions like "Who Killed the Colonel and Little Henry?" and moments like "The Madness of the Mayberry Murders."

But New Mexico is multidimensional: She has a sense of humor and can be quite tempting, with a history of outlaws, ghosts, mysterious carpenters, visitors from outer space, strange creatures that walk in the woods, and ancient bones that lay hidden.

New Mexico may never be understood, but her capriciousness and flavor can be enjoyed. Here are a few bites to tempt you.

CHAPTER ONE

The Lost Adams Gold

A dams was an exhausted man when he finally spotted the saloon. He staggered in and found himself in a barroom filled with assorted types of men. There were at least twenty who looked like former soldiers, prospectors, and desert rats. Among them was an Indian. One of the men, named John Brewer, pulled out a gold coin and ordered drinks. The Indian stepped up and said to Brewer, "If you like the gold, I know of a canyon where there is plenty." The men in the bar had a good laugh at that. How often had they heard that line? But the Indian persisted with his story, and as he laid out the details and as the drinks flowed, the men became persuaded that perhaps this time, this story was more than a mythical tale; it was a factual recounting.

The men had the time and the determination, but what they didn't have were the horses needed for an expedition of this rank. And that is where Adams came in.

Adams had arrived in the Indian village with a string of horses. He said he was a freighter and that the Apaches had originally stolen his horses. When he went after the Apaches to retrieve his livestock, the Apaches had doubled back and robbed and burned his wagons, essentially putting him out of the freighting business and leaving him with idle horses. The gold hunt was his answer. He would contribute his horses to the project if the prospectors would make him a partner. The agreement was struck, and on August 20, 1864, twenty-two men set out from Sacaton, a Pima Indian village in Arizona. They headed in a northeasterly direction following the Gila River.

Five days later, on August 25, the prospectors camped in the saddleback between Mount Ord and Mount Baldy. They were near Round Valley, now known as Springerville, Arizona. Pointing to two mountains more than a hundred miles away, the Indian told them that the gold was near those peaks.

The party descended the White Mountains and now found themselves on the east side of Round Valley. The dominating Escudilla Mountain was south of them. For the next four days they traveled toward the northeast over open country with rolling hills, mesas, and draws.

The men had been traveling for ten days, and now a suspicion was growing that their Indian guide was leading them on a pack of lies. They had been promised gold, a stream that ran nearly yellow with the stuff. All they had seen since leaving the Pima Indian camp was desert that became mountains, then rolling hills.

They had just crossed the Continental Divide. The guide made the men stop and note a poorly defined wagon road. "This," he sternly informed them, "leads to the fort in the malpais. Remember it." Why he was so adamant that the road be remembered is a mystery, unless he knew what might happen to these men alone in Apache country. That night they made camp near an old Indian agricultural patch. Adams named it "Pumpkin Patch" for the few wild melons that still grew there.

They skirted a huge plain and trudged through a large malpais, the badland, with its great expanses of lava rock. It made the traveling difficult and was exceptionally hard on the horses, and still there was no sign of gold or anything resembling it.

The next day, August 31, it took the prospectors two hours to traverse a narrow canyon that came out onto uneven ground. The guide came to a sudden halt. Pointing to two mountains that looked like sugar cones or haystacks rising in the distance, he instructed: "The *dos piloncillos* are beyond the canyon of gold."

It was the middle of the day, the sun was blistering hot, and their breath was coming hard from their climbs when the party came to what looked like a solid rock escarpment. The guide cautiously rode behind a huge boulder and disappeared; the riders followed him and found a narrow slit beyond which was a close, twisting canyon. A small stream meandered through a rocky bed on the bottom of the canyon. Because of the quick turns in the canyon, Adams called it the Zig Zag Canyon, thinking it formed a *Z*.

As the party rode along the clear stream, bright glints sparkling in the water caught the eyes of some of the men, and they dismounted, hauled out their pans, and immediately began prospecting. The glitter turned out to be gold—some of it nuggets, the size of a thumb. The prospectors had found their gold.

"No, no," insisted the Indian. "The big nuggets are in the next canyon. At the end of this canyon is a fall of water. In the next canyon you will find the real gold, the size of acorns." But gold in the hand is worth more than what might be in the next canyon. The prospectors decided to gather what they could see in front of them.

The original agreement was that the Indian guide would receive a gun, ammunition, two horses, and two gold coins when he led the prospectors to the gold. They agreed to settle up with him and send him on his way. He was more than willing to leave, and as soon as possible. He gathered his payment, nervously mounted up, and quickly left. The prospectors, now in the water with their pans, were too busy to pay much attention to his departure.

The next day the busy prospectors received a surprise visitor. Nana, chief of the Warm Springs Apaches, rode into their camp with thirty warriors. He told the miners, in fluent Spanish, that the name of the canyon was Sno-Ta-Hay. He said that they were welcome to water their horses and dig for gold, but they were not to go above the falls. The men, relieved that Nana came only to warn them and not to kill them, readily agreed.

That week, as the men mined the stream, they headed closer and closer to the end of the canyon. Greed knows no fear, and some of the men planned to go into the next canyon, and soon.

By September 10, supplies were running low, so it was decided that six of the men would go for supplies and the rest would stay, continue mining, and build a cabin. All the gold mined would be divided evenly among the group. Brewer led the contingent that went for supplies, while Adams remained with the rest. The men calculated that the trip would take a total of eight days: four days to reach the fort and get their supplies, and four days to return.

John Snively, known as the Dutchman, was uneasy. The Indians had him worried. He wanted out and elected to travel with the supply party until they came to the fort road. He was allowed to take all he had mined, which eventually was assayed at about $13,000.

The men remaining in the canyon divided their time between building a cabin and mining the stream. In the crude rock and log cabin, they built a fireplace, and under the hearthstone they stashed their gold.

On the ninth day Adams and another prospector by the name of Jack Davidson became concerned and decided to go to the head of the canyon to see if they could spot the supply group returning. What they found at the mouth of the canyon was a horrible scene: five dead men, their bodies mutilated by Apaches.

They could find neither John Brewer's body nor the Dutchman's. Evidence around the bodies indicated that the party was on its way back from getting supplies. Adams and Davidson dragged the bodies into a nearby cave and hurried to warn the miners at the camp.

They were too late. As they approached the camp, they heard Apaches yelling and whooping. Hiding in the brush, they saw a scene of devastation. Their cabin was on fire, flames shooting into the sky, and around the site were the dead bodies of their comrades.

Fear and common sense kept them hiding in the rocks and brush. After several hours, when night fell and when they were sure the Apaches had left, they headed out of the canyon. The heat of the still-smoldering cabin prevented them from trying to reclaim the gold hidden under the hearth. They would come back for that. For now, they had to be content with what they had in their pockets, a small amount of gold dust and a few nuggets.

For the next thirteen days, Davidson and Adams wandered the land, traveling only at night to avoid Apaches, drinking from streams and water holes, eating what they could scavenge from the land. Traveling at night totally disoriented them, and they were soon lost.

On the thirteenth day of their wanderings, an army patrol troop found the men, half crazed, dehydrated, and almost starved to death. The soldiers took the prospectors back to their fort, where Dr. Sturgeon, an army doctor, cared for the men until they were healthy enough to leave the post.

The Apaches were still on a rampage, and both Adams and Davidson had had enough, at least for a while. Adams returned to his family in California. Jack Davidson was an elderly man, and the ordeal was more than his health could handle. He went to Ohio, where his family lived, and died shortly thereafter.

Adams stayed away for ten years. He returned to New Mexico in 1874 and began an exhaustive search for his golden canyon. He told his story to many people, each time changing some of the details. He mounted several funded expeditions, but they always ended in failure. He just wasn't sure where the canyon was. He thought the St. Augustin Plain looked familiar, as did the countryside around Reserve. He continued telling his story and continued searching until he died in 1886. He was a man with little gold, but a lot of stories.

Meanwhile, unknown to Adams or Davidson, Snively had also made it out of the canyon. He arrived in Pinos Altos days after he split with the supply party. He had narrowly escaped the Apaches and swore he would never return to that uncivilized land. He cashed out his nuggets, returned to Arizona, and became a prosperous rancher, near Prescott. He died on his ranch in 1871, killed by Apaches.

Brewer, the leader of the supply party, was another survivor. He escaped the Apache attack on the supply party, and in 1928 his story was chronicled in the *El Paso Herald*. His account closely followed that of Adams. However, neither ever knew that the other had survived.

In late 1880 Brewer showed up at the Tenney ranch— which is twelve miles outside Round Valley, Arizona—with his Indian wife and daughter. Brewer had two freight wagons, a herd of cows, and some thoroughbred horses with him. The Tenneys offered him their hospitality, and perhaps in return, he told them the story of his trip in search of gold, twenty-five years previously.

Brewer's story is also one of adventure and horrific events. After the attack he traveled only at night, following the moon eastward. Both Adams and Davidson traveled west in their escape. Several days later, Indians from a friendly Pueblo village found Brewer. He was sick, starving, and physically and mentally exhausted. They nursed him back to health and set him on the trail to the Rio Grande. Walking down a dry riverbed, he found his way to the river and crossed over to the east side. It was here in a village, not more than a wagon stop, that he got a ride to Santa Fe on one of the wagon trains.

The Tenneys took copious notes, and along with Brewer's notes they were able to piece together the complete story for the *El Paso Herald*. Interestingly, in his narrative Brewer mentioned neither the supply party nor being part of a supply party. He told a tale of staying behind in the camp one morning to wash the dishes and tidy the camp. That was the day the Apaches attacked. He heard loud noises and, upon climbing a wall to investigate, saw the Apaches murdering the miners.

He immediately climbed higher and then ran for safety and hid in a thicket of cedars. Just before sundown he checked the area. Finding no Indians, he started out. For days he wandered, having no idea in what direction he was headed. Totally spent, he passed out by a stream. When he came to, several Indians were standing over him. He was sure his time had come. Instead, the Indians took him to their village and cared for him until he was healthy enough to make his way to the Rio Grande and find a wagon train to Santa Fe.

Of course, Tenney and Brewer, accompanied by some Round Valley men, tried to find the golden canyon. They were never able to identify all the landmarks, so their searches failed.

While there are similarities between the Adams stories and the Brewer story, there are significant discrepancies. However, Adams told his story so many times, each time a little differently, that it is hard to keep the facts straight. To add more confusion to the tale, Davidson's daughter came forward in 1929 with his journals and a map he had drawn, which showed the canyon to be in the Zuni Mountains.

Armed with all the Adams gold stories passed down from generation to generation, which can be found in diaries, notes, and newspaper stories, hundreds of amateur and professional gold hunters have tried their hand at finding the mysterious legendary gold canyon. So far none of them have succeeded.

While some basic facts can be established, there are a lot of contradictions and questions, such as exactly where the party crossed the Continental Divide, what fort they were near, in which direction they headed, and what two haystack mountains they saw. Even in the basic details there are conflicts and confusion. Some stories report that twenty men went prospecting, while other tales give the number as five or six. A few stories have the prospectors starting out from Tucson, Arizona, but most agree it was a Pima village near present-day Casa Grande, Arizona. Although almost all the stories cite New Mexico as the location of the canyon, a few say it was Arizona.

The modern treasure hunters make many claims based on their interpretations of the stories. Some calculate that the lost gold is in the Datil or Gallinas Mountains. Others point to Reserve and the Zuni Mountains. A few have insisted that they have found the site of the lost gold, but all say that the gold is gone.

Historian Paul Harden writes that he has visited the site, which is on two private ranches. He found all the landmarks and an old rock cabin, but he did not find the gold.

All the geologists who have been consulted say that there is no gold in the various areas mentioned in the stories. However, a few researchers believe that the canyon is closer to the Arizona border and farther south between Duncan, Arizona, and Cliff, New Mexico. Don Fangado, a successful hunter of lost treasures, found this site. He also found all the landmarks mentioned by Adams and the others, and this area is within the rich mineral fields around Morenci, Arizona. But here again, he found no

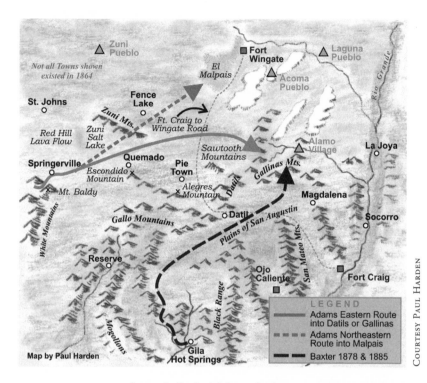

A map to the lost Adams diggings.

gold. Prospector and exhaustive researcher Jack Purcell mentions several areas, including the D-Cross Mountain area and Escondido Mountain.

Amid all the speculation and the various stories comes a very pragmatic version of the tale. Bob Lewis, onetime marshal of Magdalena, New Mexico, met Adams in Reserve in 1889. Adams wanted Lewis to guide him to the old Fort Wingate, as he believed that is where he was taken by the troopers when he was rescued. Adams hoped that, once there, the terrain would look familiar and that he could find the canyon. Unfortunately, Adams could not recognize any of the landmarks, even on the way to the old fort.

A year later Lewis and Adams would again meet, this time in a Magdalena, New Mexico, tavern. Adams complained to Lewis that the army would not escort him to the canyon so that he could bury the bodies of his slain companions, which he had left in a cave. The reality is that he was hoping that the soldiers would know the way to the canyon.

Lewis was interviewed in 1950 by historian Howard Bryan. Lewis told Bryan: "I finally located the skeletons that Adams had been talking about. They were at the mouth of a canyon about thirty-five miles northwest of Magdalena. In the canyon I also found the remains of a cabin. I found everything that Adams had described, except the gold."

Lewis believed that the gold was actually stolen from a wagon train carrying placer gold, that there were no prospectors and no Indian guide, that there was no Indian massacre, but rather that the Adams party was a bunch of thieves and murderers. They stole the gold from the wagon train, killed the wagon crew, and buried most of the money. They fled, scattering in all directions and taking what gold they could easily carry, and planned to return later to collect their loot. The times and circumstances worked against them. The Apaches and the desert collaborated to disorient them and almost kill them—and actually may have killed some men besides the four who reportedly survived.

Like most legends, the lost Adams gold produces more questions than answers. If the Indians knew of the golden canyon, why didn't they pass this information down to their descendants? If the land is now private ranch property, why haven't the ranchers recovered any of the gold as they roam the land looking for lost cattle and hunting predators? With all the hiking and off-road driving in the area, surely someone would have run across the site of the lost diggings. With satellite mappings and electronic directional findings, the site should have been easily located by treasure hunters.

After all this, if you are still interested in finding the lost Adams gold, you might want to start at a place called Adams Diggings, New Mexico. In 1916 Guy and Daisy Magee came to the rolling hills north of, and in between, Pie Town and Quemado, where they homesteaded a piece of land. In 1920 they established a small general store for the nearby ranchers. When the stock market crashed in 1929, people were looking for a way to make a living, and the adventuresome sort went treasure hunting. The Adams digging stories were in wide circulation, so these men went prospecting armed with maps, newspaper articles, and a couple of brochures.

Because many people at the time thought that the golden canyon was located in the general area of Pie Town and Quemado, the gold hunters arrived in droves. They got their supplies at the Magees' store. Some wanted to mail letters, or receive mail, so the Magees applied to establish a post office. The name

COURTESY MIKE MARRIOTT

Adams Diggings, a stop on the road to Adams's gold in the distant mountains.

they submitted was Adams Diggings, partly to identify the post office's location and partly as a gimmick.

The name was approved, and the small spot was named. You can still find it on a New Mexico map. After World War II the flow of prospectors dwindled, and now only a few come through this rural spot. All are looking for either the gold or the history. No one who has come here has ever found the lost gold, or any gold, but since so many stories point in this direction, it could be close.

CHAPTER TWO

The Disappearance of a People

The valley was sixteen miles long, and most of the rain that fell from the heavens around it fell on the valley. Bleak winters promised snow and temperatures as low as 20 degrees below zero. Summer was just as punishing, with roasting temperatures, sometimes hovering around 100 degrees, and no rain to cool the air. It could be freezing cold and bleak; it could be unbearably hot and dry. That was Chaco Canyon.

The Chaco world was inhabited by rattlesnakes, badgers, horned toads, whip snakes, bull snakes, lizards, and ravens, as well as wild turkeys, owls, desert cottontails, jackrabbits, coyotes, antelope, bear, and deer. There was game to eat, and plenty of danger from the wildlife.

The area never received more than nine inches of rain a year, and often less. Water was almost never found in Chaco Wash, although it was eight feet wide and one and a half feet deep, with cottonwoods growing on its banks. An inhospitable land, it was home to about 5,000 people.

A.D. 1100

The wind rode the dry ground at a steady, strong pace, whipping up swirls of dust as it moved. There had been a lot of wind lately, the boy knew it well, and being a boy, he treated it with mischievous competition, racing it from point to point. "If I get to the rock before the wind, I will win riches," thought the boy. "If I get to the watering ditch before the wind, I will be strong," wished the boy. "If I get to the wall before the wind, I will be brave," murmured the boy. It was an ageless game to be played by children through eternity.

The wind was a worthy opponent, keeping pace, sometimes leading the way, sometimes falling behind, but always there; it kept up a steady taunting, whistling, and howling as it pushed along. But the boy did not mind. He had heard the wind for many years, but now it was stronger and, he thought, more daring. The field where his people toiled over the corn and beans was now a floor of hard caliches. The wind had stripped the growing sand off and taken it away— exactly where, the child did not know.

He remembered that in the past his family would search for the new place the wind had hidden the sand, and then they would start their crops over. Sometimes they had to dig new water ditches, and sometimes they even had to move and build a new house. But this time he knew it was different. No one had found the land that was blown away. Maybe that was why the elders were in the kiva. Maybe they were asking the gods to tell them where the land went.

The boy was late. His mother had sent him to pick the few remaining ears of corn. The crop had been poor this year, even worse than last year. It was the rains. Each year there was less and less rain. Each year the wash ran lower, and each year the irrigation ditches were shallower. Maybe that was why the elders were in the great kiva. Maybe they were making sacrifices to the rain gods.

He had to hurry. If he was too late, he would never find out any important news. It was his brother who always told him things. But now his brother was gone. He had taken a mate and moved to her mother's house. Such was the way of his people. Mothers were important. They controlled the family, the wealth, and the crops. Mothers made important decisions. The boy knew that when he found a mate, he too would move into her home. But not yet—he was too young.

First he would learn to be a good warrior. His people needed him. It was told that a long time ago strangers came and moved into their homes. Then came a time when they all worked together. But maybe more people were coming to kill his neighbors; maybe he would have to fight and be a brave warrior. Perhaps that was why the elders were in the kiva—to pray to the gods for strength to defeat the enemy.

His pueblo was only one of many in the area. Some were close by; others, not too far. He thought his pueblo was the most beautiful, a *pueblo bonito*. It had many, many rooms, at least eight hundred of them.

His mother often told him how lucky he was. He lived in a powerful and important religious place. His mother told him that many smaller pueblos were controlled by his pueblo. He had never seen them. But he knew that much wealth came to his home: beautiful birds from far south, seashells from a mysterious water, and the most precious of all, turquoise.

The boy was also taught that he must be obedient. His home was the most powerful, and if he disobeyed, he would be swiftly and viciously punished. With his own eyes he had seen what happened to those who disobeyed. They were killed and sometimes beheaded. Sometimes the elders even ate their flesh to totally conquer their evil. These thoughts made the boy hurry to his pueblo, but not because he was afraid.

He knew the pueblos were very strong. It was difficult to enter one without being observed. They had no outside doors or courtyard gates. Even most of the windows and some ventilation slots had been closed over. He didn't know when this had happened, for he had never seen open windows on the square or doors on the outer wall. But he did know that it was for protection from the outside world. All the surrounding pueblos had similar security. There was someone, or something, that the families feared.

The boy scampered up a ladder and ran along the rooftops. The boy had no fear now, only puzzlement. The important elders were gone from the pueblos. They were meeting in the Great Kiva that stood by itself down in the canyon. They had been there all day, and in a way that worried him. Something very important must be happening.

As he hurried along the rooftops, he passed women grinding corn with stones or cooking food on flat stones. One woman was carefully painting a bold black-and-white design on a new pot. Several naked children played their games on the rooftops under the watchful eyes of their mothers.

He climbed another ladder and then dropped down to the coolness of his family's rooms. He left the wind outside, howling its displeasure. The thick walls of his home protected his family from the harsh wind, and the heat and rain.

The room he was in was just like its neighbors. It was a barren room furnished with only thin rush sleeping mats, which were now rolled off to the side. His mother was not in the main room, so he checked the storage rooms. The first storage room held a clothes pole with a blanket, a bed covering, and a tanned hide. His father's turkey-feather robe hung from a wooden peg.

He found his mother in the second storage room. She was kneeling in the corner, facing the wall. She turned quickly, startled by his entrance. He saw that she had carefully laid out the family's prized possession, the turquoise necklace made from 2,500 beads. With it were four turquoise earrings shaped like large rectangles. Over the years he had seen his mother and sister painstakingly craft the beads, first rubbing them with a stone, then piercing them so that they could be strung.

It was a prized possession proclaiming not only the skill of the family but also its wealth and social standing. His mother turned back to the carefully laid-out jewelry and covered it with sand.

Turning to her son, she ordered him not to tell anyone what he had just seen. He must keep the secret from family and friends. Not understanding, but being obedient, he promised he would say nothing. But it was all very strange to the boy—the disappearing land, the important meeting of the elders, and now his mother's unusual behavior with the family wealth.

1921

The sandstorm rolled down the canyon, propelled by a wind that was determined to coat everything with fine particles. When the sandstorm had passed, Neil Judd noticed that the sand permeated the tents, the tools, clothes, and even the food. Sometimes the wind howled, sometimes it whispered, but it was a constant companion.

Judd and his archaeological team had been sent by the National Geographic Society to study Pueblo Bonito and its immediate neighbor, Pueblo del Arroyo. He wrote back to the Society: "This expedition hopes to discover the historic secrets of a region which was one of the most densely populated areas in North America before Columbus came, a region where prehistoric peoples lived in vast communal dwellings whose ruins are ranked second to none of ancient times in point of architecture and whose customs, ceremonies, and name have been engulfed in . . . oblivion."

The excavation of Pueblo Bonito revealed many mysteries. The first mystery the team encountered was the placement of artifacts. In a dig the land becomes a calendar, with newer artifacts lying above older ones, and archaeologists had come to rely on the dating of pottery to determine the age of a ruin. However, the deeper Judd's group dug, the newer the pottery was. Old shards lay on top of newer ones. It took Judd four years to solve the mystery. Apparently, the pueblo builders had dug beneath an old village to build the foundation of their newer one. As they excavated, they threw out dirt containing old pottery shards, which then lay over more recently discarded pottery bits.

The topsy-turvy diggings were only one of the mysteries the archaeologists encountered. The lack of burial sites was another. For a site that covered as much land and as many ruins as Chaco Canyon, the bones of thousands of people should have been uncovered. However, the skeletons were few and far between. Eventually, over the years and with an exhaustive survey by amateur and professional archaeologists, it was determined that seven hundred skeletons might be on the site. Still the number seemed small for the size of the ruin.

Another puzzle was water. Signs of irrigation ditches and tilled soil revealed a sophisticated system of flood agriculture. This part of the Southwest was desert, the rains were mostly monsoon, and water was a precious commodity. Water for cooking and daily living needs had to be transported up ladders and down into dwellings. Daily life was hard work.

With meticulous surveying and digging, the National Geographic Society team was able to identify and describe several more great houses. Pueblo Una Vida was 994 feet around and built of very fine-grained tabular sandstone. Debris indicated that it was more than two stories high. It had four circular kivas.

A mile down the canyon stood the ruins of Hungo Pavi. It was 872 feet around and had 72 rooms on its ground level. One kiva was built in the middle.

Beyond this lay the ruins of Chetro Ketl. It was an imposing structure at least 1,300 feet in circumference. A first floor of 124 rooms was surrounded at its base with what looked like the rubble of perhaps three stories. This great house had six circular kivas. Chetro Ketl measured more than 1,500 feet in circumference and formed an *E*. It was estimated that more than 50 million pieces of stone went into building its walls. It had several kivas, but the most surprising find for Judd was the huge circular depression that proved to be a ceremonial ring.

Pueblo Bonito lay 600 yards away from Chetro Ketl. This was the main ruin Judd chose to excavate. Its perimeter was 1,300 feet, and it stood at least four stories high. The ground floor held 139 rooms. Pueblo Bonito was east of the ruin of Pueblo del Arroyo, which had a perimeter of 1,000 feet.

The last ruin the excavation group identified was Pueblo de Penasca Blanco, which was situated two miles down the canyon. This pueblo had been built in the form of a circle.

One of the most exciting finds was Casa Rinconada, across from the Chaco Wash. This was a large kiva, and the only ruin to stand completely by itself. This great kiva was 63.5 feet across at floor level. It contained a bench built around its circumference. Unlike the other kivas, it had a subterranean passage that descended four steps and ran in a straight line across the floor of the kiva, then turned slightly, passed under the bench, and rose to the level of the first antechamber. A series of steps then led to the second antechamber. The archaeologists speculated that this allowed the priests to enter and leave the kiva without being seen so that they could miraculously appear to the people on the benches.

Over the next five years, Judd and his crew revealed a society more advanced than they initially thought. A series of roads were discovered that tied together not only the pueblos in Chaco Canyon but also outliers that covered more than 38,000 square miles.

When the dig was finished, Judd found that he had more questions than answers. He never found the Chaco burial site; he wasn't sure of the exact purpose of this ancient city; and he still didn't know where the people had gone and when they had left. What he did know was that they had inhabited one of the largest, most powerful ancient sites in America.

1999

Stephen Lekson was still looking for answers to the mystery of Chaco Canyon. As curator of anthropology at the University Museum, University of Colorado, Boulder, he had just finished working on a Chacoan "outlier" ruin in Utah. His work only intensified his curiosity about the main center, Chaco. The roads that fanned out from Chaco were wide and well constructed, and some had curbs. They cut through hills, and a few were built with retaining walls. There is also evidence of way stations and a footbridge across an arroyo. These roads provided a means for food, as well as the large ponderosa pines that made up the beams in the rooms, to be brought to Chaco. They may even have served as highways for trade. Spaced along the routes were watchtowers.

Though the Chaco population was estimated to be no more than 5,000, the physical presence of the place indicated that it was something more than a large pueblo. Its influence was far-reaching, and as such it was more of a political and religious center. Chaco contained a great house with public buildings, warehouses, and palaces in a large city that encompassed four square miles.

Questions remain as to where the Chacoans came from. Chaco did not just rise alone from the desert sand. Similar sites were produced after the end of Chaco in other geographic locations. However, the structure of Chaco—with its complex and sophisticated irrigation system with dams, ditches, and holding areas, as well as the roadways—defines an advanced civilization. A civilization that could create such an infrastructure should have left footprints on its way to, and away from, Chaco.

Such a large, wealthy complex should have been the target of invasions and war. Yet there is little evidence of strife at Chaco. Lekson believed that the Chacoans kept the peace by violent means. Cruel punishment was meted out for breaking rules, and trophy skulls have been found among the ruins. What the archaeologist did discover was evidence that when Chaco finally fell, it was during a violent time marked by wars. It faced turmoil and attacks.

Some researchers think that a devastating drought caused the fall of Chaco and caused an Aztec site to be built someplace else on an unoccupied spot in a valley of little importance. There is a connection in time that would argue for this continuance. But that would mean a dynasty had been created. This was unknown and unheard of in the ancient Southwest. Yet it is hard to believe that a people who developed an extensive system of irrigation, and built roads covering thousands of miles, did nothing to protect their vast empire.

While the demise of Chaco is still a mystery, the fall of the later site at Aztec, New Mexico, is not. Proof exists that the end of Aztec was caused by the Great Drought, which scientists have dated to about 1275. This coincides with the demise of Aztec.

Lekson believed that the political order of Chaco was continued by Aztec from A.D. 1125 to 1275, which was then followed by Paquime or Casas Grandes. The Aztec ruins are north of Chaco, but Paquime is located in a fertile river valley in northern Chihuahua, Mexico. Paquime was built around the time archaeologists think that Aztec ended.

While the excavation of Paquime has shown it to be a wealthier site than Chaco, it did not seem to carry the strong political influence wielded by the latter.

Has Lekson answered the mystery of Chaco and its people? Did the people of Chaco abandon their glorious city because of a drought? Did war cause the end of this great political center? Or was it such a violent culture that the people rebelled? When a regime is powerful and oppressive, it breeds revolution. Is it possible that the people of Chaco rose up and destroyed their government and their city, building their new city in Aztec? Or was it a peaceful exodus to a new home? Was it a great exodus, or did they migrate over time? Was the land plagued by warfare after Chaco fell?

If Chaco was a stifling culture, it is possible that over time people left to found their own pueblo. It is only natural that they would take their cultural traditions with them. The architecture of Aztec is very similar to that of Chaco, and artifacts show that the way of life was also similar.

Chaco shows signs of being a great ceremonial center. Paquime was a commercial center, and Aztec seemed to bridge the two. Together they produced a pattern of the prehistoric Southwest that still presents unsolved mysteries to the world.

No one knows when the people of these pueblos arrived in these lands; no one knows when they left, and it is only speculation on where they went. But everyone knows they were here. They left their signature on rocks with mystical drawings, bits and pieces of beautifully crafted pottery, and gravity-defying dwellings that clung to cliff edges.

CHAPTER THREE

La Llorona: The Weeping Woman

It was saint's day in Pojoaque. Not just any saint's day, but a day of celebration for the patron saint of the village church, and it was a good day for Stephen. He had no chores that day, he didn't have any schoolwork, and best of all neither did his friends, which is why they were all running around together at the fiesta.

A High Mass was offered, but that did not affect Stephen, since he hardly ever attended church. His parents were not religious. It was only when someone died that he found himself sitting in front of the ornate altar painted with saints and angels. Those were important days for a nine-year-old because when there was a funeral, he didn't have to go to school.

Today the celebration included a parade and entertainment by the town musicians. The priest led the people in a walk around the church, his gilded censer swinging slowly back and forth. As he blessed the path with holy water, a procession of townspeople and church members followed him around and around the small old church. During this procession the Native Americans from the nearby pueblo solemnly beat their drums, adding their cadence to the religious walk.

The town was dressed in banners, and some old-timers added to the festivities by shooting off their blunderbusses in the town square. For a few moments after their volley, black smoke would hang in the air. As soon as that cleared, the old-timers would load the black powder in their old guns and—Boom! Boom!—fill the air with black smoke again. The sound and the smoke continued all day, adding to the excitement of the festival.

Every time the guns went off, Stephen and his friends would run around, their hands over their ears, yelling and rolling on the ground as they pretended they had been shot. They were rowdy and foolish as only nine-year-old boys can be.

As evening approached, the churchwomen came laden with food from their kitchens. Some of them arrived in horse and buggies, while others walked, carrying their precious gifts of food. The cooking had started the day before, and all the Mexican food favorites were offered to the glory of their saint and for the pleasure of their neighbors. As dusk fell, the luminaries were lit, casting a soft glow around the church and the people. Replete with food and content with the day, the adults settled in to swap gossip and stories. All ears and big-eyed, the children sat around the elders and were given sage advice such as "A hooting owl means the dead are rising from their grave" or "Don't go into the graveyard at night because the dead will pull your toes."

With these delightfully frightening stories rumbling around in their heads, more than half a dozen young boys headed for the cottonwoods near the river. Suddenly they heard the hoot of an owl. They stopped in their tracks, thinking it was the call of the dead rising. They stood as still as statues, listening to that call, when all of a sudden the call changed from a hollow hooting to a wailing cry. The boys looked around for the weeping creature.

The smoke from the fires had drifted down to the river, laying a soft gray film over the water and its surrounding banks. And then suddenly they saw her, through the smoky haze, a woman dressed in black, her head covered with a veil. The lights from the lamps on the hill sifted down to the riverbank, outlining her slight figure.

She slowly turned away from the river and headed up the hill, walking toward the cemetery and continuing her plaintive cries. The sight of the figure headed for the cemetery was all the boys needed. They shot forward as fast as their legs would propel them and ran straight back to the adults and the luminaries, back to the light and their parents and neighbors and family.

Their shaken state was obvious to the elders. After hearing the children's story, the elders told one of their own, the story of La Llorona, the weeping woman, for surely that was who the children saw.

La Llorona! The weeping woman. Her story had been told for decades to young boys and girls. It is an important folktale of the Hispanic culture, and there are many versions and descriptions of La Llorona. The common thread is that the children of a beautiful woman died and she seeks them for eternity, her pitiful cries filling the air as she searches.

Some say she was a peasant who was unhappy with her lowly state. She was a woman of exquisite beauty who dreamed of riches, a handsome husband, and an honored place in society. One day she met such a man, and he gave her the riches she desired. Some versions of the story say that they were married, while others say that they only lived together. She bore him two children, and as the years passed, he became disenchanted with her. She grew older, and her beauty began to fade.

Her handsome lover gave her less and less attention. He stayed away for long periods and came home without apology, only to wander off again. She was so worried that she was losing him that she started to lose weight. She began questioning him and often complained. He found her looks and ways becoming less and less attractive.

According to one version, she and her children were walking by the river when a fine carriage came up and stopped. Inside was her lover with a pretty young woman. He talked to the children, completely ignoring their mother, and then drove away. In a fit of rage and jealousy, the mother decided to rid herself of the children. Then perhaps he would notice her again. The river was nearby; she led them into the waters and drowned them.

Of course, her lover never came back. Filled with grief and loss, she searched the waters, calling to her children, tears of remorse and sorrow cascading down her face. But the children never answered, and so she is doomed to walk the riverbanks, forever seeking her children.

Another popular version tells the story of a poor beautiful woman who had two children. At night she would leave the children to go dancing. She was much admired, and many men wanted to marry her, but they did not know about the children. Realizing that no rich man would marry a woman with children, regardless of how beautiful she was, she decided to rid herself of the children. She left them by the river, telling them not to move until she came back. When the river rose, the obedient children stayed on the riverbank and drowned.

After she walked away from the children, she realized what she had done. She loved her children, perhaps more than riches, so she ran back to the river, but the children were gone. The river had washed them away. She raced up and down the river, calling out to them and crying in pain, but there was no sign of them. And so she walks the riverbanks, seeking her children and crying.

La Llorona will seek any child, and if she finds a child near the river during her nightly search, she will snatch the child away. Some say she drowns the children, while some say she just makes them disappear.

There is no universal description of La Llorona. Although most admit she is beautiful, she has also been described as no more than four feet tall and with a beak and warts, or a skeleton face. One man who saw her said that her skin was like leather and her eyes were a flaming red. Usually La Llorona is dressed in white, but sometimes she appears in black. Her face is always covered with a veil.

The legend of La Llorona is often told to children who are misbehaving. "If you do not listen to your mother, La Llorona will come for you." But La Llorona has influenced more than misbehaving children.

Phillip, for one, decided to go to the bar and not to church on Good Friday. His wife, afraid he would be cursed, pleaded with him to accompany her to the service. Phillip ignored her pleas and headed for the saloon. He stayed there all day, enjoying the company of other "sinners," and it was late at night when he finally headed home.

As he neared his home, which stood on a street near the river, he heard the cries of a woman. Turning, he saw a figure all in white pointing a bony finger at him. Phillip spun around and took off. In his haste to flee, he tripped over his own feet and went down hard. He looked around, fearful that the woman was coming for him, but she was gone.

Shaken, he hurried home. When he reached his house, he saw a baby wrapped in a white blanket in his driveway. Reaching down, he picked up the infant and pulled the blanket from its face. The baby had huge, dark eyes and a penetrating stare; her teeth were white and sharp. And then a bony hand came out of the blanket and pointed at him. He dropped the blanket, ran into his house, and never took another drink.

La Llorona is credited with more than just curing drunks. One family tells a story of how, in 1865, she appeared to a young man who refused to bathe. The family was beside itself trying to convince this young man that a bath was necessary. They finally banished him to the fields because he smelled so bad. One night as he sat alone under the moonlight, La Llorona approached him and threatened to scrub his skin off if he did not take a bath. From that day on until he died, he bathed every week.

The weeping woman legend is not just from the distant past. In 1953 a man was driving home late at night and picked up what he thought was a Catholic nun walking along the road-side. He stopped to pick her up; she entered the car but said nothing.

During the drive he tried to make conversation, but she never answered and never looked at him. She just faced straight ahead. The young man became uncomfortable, and the thought of robbery or even murder entered his mind. Then he noticed the smell of sulfur. He pulled the car over and turned to tell her to leave, but she had disappeared. The night was pierced with a blood-curdling yell that raised the hackles on the back of his neck. The next night he told a friend of his encounter. "The same thing happened to another man a few weeks ago," Freddie said. "That was La Llorona."

In most of the tales about La Llorona, she strikes terror into the hearts of children and adults, causing them to behave better—to take baths, or stop drinking, or mind their mothers.

In one tale she even cures a cheating husband of his wanderings. Ramon enjoyed the company of many women. His wife was not the jealous type but was unhappy with his roving eye. One night she warned him, "If you go out tonight, something is going to happen to you." Ignoring her comment as that of a complaining wife, he left to enjoy his night of dancing and drinking.

As he was heading home in the early-morning hours, he spotted a very attractive woman walking in front of him. He caught up to her, and turning her around to face him, he pulled her veil aside, deciding that perhaps he would give her a kiss. But what he saw was the skeleton face of La Llorona lit by the moon. He never cheated on his wife again.

While most of the La Llorona tales are shocking or frightening, a few tales are humorous. In 1970 a group of hippies settled in Chimayo, New Mexico. Most of them were respectful and kept to themselves, but Crow was different. He dressed in an Indian breechcloth, his neck adorned with beads and feathers. He rode his horse through his neighbors' pastures and gardens, always leaving gates wide open because he believed in freeing the animals into the wild. He thought the land belonged to everyone, and he honored no fences or gates.

The villagers found vegetables and fruit missing from their gardens and orchards, but no one could prove who was taking them. Crow was suspected, but complaining to him did no good. In frustration, some folks would even fire a shot off in his direction. However, nothing daunted Crow.

It was October, the weather had been particularly mild, and there were still vegetables in the gardens. It was late at night, but Mrs. Martinez was having trouble sleeping. Her sciatica was bothering her, and the banging sound of the wind blowing the loose tin on her roof kept her awake. She decided a hot drink would help and headed for her kitchen.

She was sitting in the dark, looking at the bright moon lighting up her garden, which was near a large irrigation ditch. Suddenly she thought she saw a shadow moving in her garden. As she peered into the night, the moonlight illuminated a figure that was stealthily making its way through the rows of vegetables. He would bend here and there as if he were picking up something. She realized he was pulling up her carrots and placing them in the sack he carried on his back. Seeing his breechcloth, she knew it was Crow.

Suddenly the wind picked up and started howling louder and louder. Then she knew it was not the wind making the noise. She saw La Llorona floating across the ditch, dressed in black, and the specter's howling increased as she advanced toward Crow. Crow straightened at the noise; his eyes grew big as La Llorona came toward him. He dropped the bag, carrots and all, and ran. He was in such a rush that he fell on the fence. Scrabbling, he couldn't get up, so he continued on all fours, running away from the garden and La Llorona. However, as he ran along the road, the howling followed him. Porch lights came on in the houses he passed, and dogs set up a clamor, which made his escape obvious to all. Crow never stole Mrs. Martinez's carrots again.

The legend and stories of La Llorona can be found everywhere from Mexico to Spain, from South America to North America. However, if you had to pick a home for La Llorona, it would have to be in Santa Fe, New Mexico, for it is here that she seems to have settled in.

The Public Employees Retirement Association (PERA) building was constructed on the grounds of an old cemetery that is near a large irrigation ditch. It is now filled with government offices and state employees. When the officials decided to construct the building on the grounds of the old Catholic cemetery, they dug up the bodies and buried them somewhere else. This building is now the home of La Llorona. She roams the halls at night, turning the lights off and on. Some workers have actually seen her during the day, and the cleaning crews hear her slamming doors and crying for her lost children. Sometimes they hear her feet as she climbs the back steps. Yet when they look, no one is there. At other times, she is seen walking down one of the halls, dressed in black, her face covered by the ubiquitous veil.

Eduardo was employed as a nighttime cleaning man and had just finished scrubbing the long marble hallway in the PERA building when his wife arrived with his dinner. "Do not forget to bring the dishes home," she admonished him. "You always forget."

He returned to the hallway, sat on his stool in front of a small electric heater, and unwrapped his dinner. He heard someone say "Darkness," and the electric heater and the lights went off. Seconds later the lights came back on, only to go off again when a woman sharply said "Darkness."

Eduardo felt something brush past him. He grabbed his flashlight and hurried down the hall, shining the light on the walls and floor of the hallway. There, in front of him, he saw a woman with long black hair holding a black shawl to her face. He heard her whimper as she continued to move down the hall. Then she faded away.

The night was very cold when Eduardo ran out of the PERA building. He looked back just as the doors flew open and two balls of fire shot out of the building, heading straight for him. He wasted no time in running home. When Eduardo arrived home, his wife wanted to know why he had forgotten the dishes again.

While La Llorona is very much a part of the Hispanic folklore culture, other cultures also tell of a weeping woman who has lost her children. It is an ancient tale, appearing even in the Bible. In Matthew 2:18 it is written: "In Rama was there a voice heard, lamentation, and weeping, and great mourning, Rachel weeping for her children, and would not be comforted, because they are not."

The ancient Aztec Indians heard the screams of their earth goddess, and various Celtic tales tell of a weeping woman. When the conquistador Hernán Cortés informed his mistress that he was heading back to Spain with their son, but not her, she pierced her son's heart and her own with an obsidian knife. Her cries were heard for centuries.

The tale of the weeping woman is carried from country to country and century to century, but it seems to be a favorite in Hispanic cultures. Its moral is universal and warns listeners to value what they have. It also preaches the timeless advice of "Be careful what you wish for." La Llorona's wishes came true, and with them came a sorrow that carries through the ages.

CHAPTER FOUR

Who Killed the Colonel and Little Henry?

It was a game of politics, power, and enough greed to turn it deadly. The major players were men of cruel character, an avenger on a mission, and a small boy. The sides were divided: Republicans against Democrats, stock growers against rustlers. But when the political maneuvering was done, when the citizen pressure reached its peak, and when the evidence was gathered, nothing was solved. The disappearance of the Fountains remained a mystery.

Albert J. Fountain inspired either admiration or hatred. He was a man of note in Lincoln County and in the New Mexico Territory. He was known for defending Billy the Kid and Dan Tucker on murder charges, and he was a civic leader who founded the *Mesilla Valley Independent* newspaper.

In his youth, as a reporter for the *Sacramento Union*, Fountain went to Nicaragua to cover the William Walker expedition. There, he was arrested, sentenced to death, and escaped dressed as a woman.

COURTESY PALACE OF THE GOVERNORS PHOTO ARCHIVES (NMHM/DCA) #9873

Colonel Albert Jennings Fountain in his militia uniform.

After studying law for two years, he passed the California State Bar. Then, with war threatening to rip apart the United States in 1861, he enlisted in the First California Infantry Volunteers. He saw action against the Apaches and moved up the ranks quickly, leaving the California Volunteers as a lieutenant in 1864.

On one particular mission with his partner Corporal Val Sanchez, he headed out to seek the Apaches, but he found himself separated from Sanchez and cornered in a narrow pass.

He spent the night alone, with arrows in his shoulder and fore-arm, trapped under his dead horse. His partner made it to Fort McRae, and Fountain was rescued the next day. It was another brush with death for Fountain, and his escape convinced him that he was impervious to danger. That thinking was to make him both incautious and more firmly set on his paths of justice.

The Fountain family had been living in Texas, where Fountain served four years as a senator and helped in the read-mission of Texas to the Union in 1870. A strong supporter of law and order, he reactivated the Texas Rangers.

Three years later the Fountain family, which included Albert, his wife Mariana, and their five children, moved to Mesilla, New Mexico. He brought with him his righteous ways. He established a law practice and was eventually appointed an assistant U.S. district attorney. Always a strong believer in the military—its strict discipline, order, and structure appealed to his frame of mind and his high values of honesty and hard work—he joined the Mesilla Scouts as a captain and by 1883 achieved the rank of colonel.

Set on the path of cleaning up the lawlessness and corrup-tion in the territory, he took on the Santa Fe Ring. The Ring, a group of politicians led by Thomas Catron, was more inter-ested in acquiring wealth and land holdings for themselves than in working for the good of the citizens. By controlling federal patronage and favors through the territorial government, they managed to build a power base that was uncontested. Fountain also took on Albert B. Fall. Taking on the Santa Fe Ring was courageous; taking on Albert Fall proved deadly.

Fountain first met Fall at the Las Cruces Free Mason Lodge, where both were members. Their relationship at first was cautious but then turned bitter. Fountain, a feisty Republican, and Fall, a dedicated Democrat, locked heads over a New Mexico legislature seat. Fountain won, became Speaker of the House, and worked ceaselessly for statehood. Statehood meant law and order and reporting to a higher authority, but it also meant a loss of local power—none of which were in Fall's best interest.

There was a remarkable contrast between Fountain and Fall. Fountain was an educated man who had served in the military as an officer, had studied law, and was known as a family man. A religious man, he helped establish St. Clement's Church. An ardent civic leader, he established the *Mesilla Valley Independent* newspaper.

Fall was a miner who described himself as a "cowboy, lawyer, judge, gunfighter, able editor, farmer, rough rider, cavalier, and brevet captain of industry." He founded the Las Cruces *Independent Democrat*, a newspaper with strong Democratic Party leanings. Fountain's Mesilla newspaper definitely presented Republican views. The two were at opposite ends of the political and personal spectrum.

In 1890 Fall and Fountain faced off for a legislative seat, which Fall won by forty-five votes. In the 1892 elections the Republicans sent the militia in to guard the polls. Fall retaliated by calling on his friend Oliver Lee to lead armed men into town. Fall contended that the militia was there to intimidate the voters, and he wanted to protect them. Fall was reelected. When he was made district judge, he appointed Oliver Lee, James Gililland, and William McNew U.S. deputy marshals. The bitterness between Fall and Fountain grew into hatred.

New Mexico was long overdue for statehood, but its reputation for rampant lawlessness was keeping it from being admitted to the Union. Concerned New Mexicans wanted corruption eliminated and the lawlessness in the territory contained.

The biggest crime in the territory was cattle rustling, and by 1894 the ranchers had finally had enough. They formed the Southeastern New Mexico Stock Growers' Association. Fountain was appointed their special investigator and lawyer. He was helped by Ben Williams, a Las Cruces constable, and Les Dow, a U.S. marshal. Fountain went after rustlers with the aggressiveness he was known for, and before the year was out, he and his assistants had sent twenty rustlers to the penitentiary.

In the 1894 sheriff's election, a strange thing happened. Eighty-eight ballots disappeared, finally showing up after lunch at the post office. With these votes Guadalupe Ascarate, the Democratic candidate, was elected. The Republicans appealed the election, but it was not settled until it was too late for Fountain and his family. Having a Democratic sheriff in a contested election proved to have a significant effect on the investigation into the disappearance of the Fountains.

Fountain was hot on the trail of a gang of rustlers that included William McNew. That's when the threats came to Fountain. But this fearless man who had faced warring Apaches, foreign armies, and almost a firing squad was undaunted. He persevered in his investigations and goals. He had enough evidence on McNew and his companions to convict them of cattle stealing and altering brands.

On January 12, 1896, Fountain left for the county seat in Lincoln to meet with a grand jury to secure indictments against the rustlers. Mariana, his wife, was worried about his safety and insisted that he take Henry, their eight-year-old son, with him.

In Lincoln, Fountain presented his documents and letters to the court and was rewarded with thirty-two indictments against twenty-three men, including William McNew and Oliver Lee, Fall's compatriots.

Albert Fountain triumphantly stood on the steps of the Lincoln County courthouse, waving a fistful of papers. Next to him his eight-year-old son pranced about, anxious to start his trip home. Henry didn't understand why he had to come with his father anyway. It sounded like a real adventure at first, but as the days wore on and his father "took care of business" in Lincoln, Henry became bored.

Henry was too young to understand that there was a very important reason for him to accompany his father. Fountain was an aggressive avenger, and his life had been threatened, but his family felt that the presence of little Henry would forestall any attempts on Fountain's life. Who would be so cruel as to hurt a small helpless boy?

The crowd around Fountain was made up of ranchers, cowboys, and various minor politicians. Suddenly a slip of paper was thrust into Fountain's hand. He unfolded the scrap and read: "If you drop this, we will be your friends. If you go on with it, you will never reach home alive."

Attorney George Pritchard, who was standing next to Fountain, read the words in the note. He took them seriously and urged Fountain to remain in Lincoln overnight so that he could travel with the mail carrier the next day.

Fountain would have no part of what he considered a cowardly way out and one that would appease the outlaws. He gathered up Henry and their belongings and headed west for home. It was a bitterly cold January. Ice and snow covered the ground, and Fountain knew it would be a long and uncomfortable trip, especially for Henry. It would take three days and two nights to get home.

The first night the Fountains stopped at Blazer's Mill. Joseph Blazer, an old friend of Fountain's, was interested in the court proceeding, and when told about the note, he showed concern. He too urged Fountain to wait until someone could ride with him. But Fountain's bravado and false sense of security demanded that he continue on.

Before they started out the next day, an Apache friend gave Fountain a pony to cover part of a loan. Fountain thanked him, knowing that the children would be thrilled, including Henry, who was eyeing the pony with delight. The pony was tied to the back of the buckboard, and the Fountains headed out for their next night's stop. Along the way Fountain noticed two men who seemed to be following him, but they were too far away for him to recognize them.

That night they stayed at David Sutherland's home in La Luz. Hoping to cheer up Henry, his father gave him a quarter to spend in Sutherland's store. Henry bought 10 cents' worth of candy and then carefully wrapped the dime and nickel change in the corner of his handkerchief.

The next morning the weather was worse, and Henry, wrapped up in his Indian blanket, sat huddled close to his father. Still, it was too cold for the child, and Fountain wanted to hurry home.

On Saturday, when Fountain and little Henry started their last leg of the journey, it was freezing and windy. Only the thought of home kept them moving in that miserable weather.

Now Fountain noted three horsemen trailing him, but they were too far away for him to see them clearly. Sometimes they were ahead of him, sometimes behind, but always with him. He noticed that one of the horses was white and the other two were darker. Also, one rider wore a black hat.

Before noon the Fountains met mail carrier Santos Alvarado. They spoke briefly. Alvarado did notice the riders and later testified that he had seen them along the road, but too far away to be identified.

The Fountains stopped for lunch at Pellman's Well and, after a brief rest, continued their journey west, past White Sands. That afternoon they met five riders about two and a half miles from Chalk Hill. One of the riders, Saturnino Barela, was a mail carrier whom Fountain knew quite well. Their conversation soon turned to the three riders. The riders, who were about a quarter of a mile away, turned from the road when they saw the other travelers. Only the color of the horses could be identified from that distance.

Fountain was uneasy, and Barela suggested that he turn back to the mail station, stop overnight, and travel the next day with Barela when he headed west on his mail route. Fountain thought about it but decided it was best to hurry home as Henry had come down with a cold and needed his mother's care. Knowing that Mariana would be worried about them, he continued on his journey home.

The next morning Barela started out with the mail, heading toward La Cruces and traveling over the trail where he had met the Fountains. Five miles beyond the point where he and Fountain had conversed, he spotted buckboard tracks turning off the road. He followed the tracks for about thirty or forty yards and noticed the tracks of three other horses around the buckboard. Barela was concerned for the Fountains. He decided to check their home to see if they had made it back safely. However, when he reached the Fountain home, he learned that they had not returned.

Fountain's oldest son, Albert, immediately formed a posse with his brother Jack, his father-in-law, and several townspeople. They set out for Chalk Hill, the last place the colonel and Henry had been seen. It was a bitter ride in the howling winter wind.

Later that evening about twenty-five men formed another posse. This one included Dona Ana County Sheriff Captain Eugene Van Patten and Captain Thomas Branigan.

The next morning the posses joined forces and thoroughly searched the area around Chalk Hill. Near the area where the buckboard had turned off the road, impressions in the ground revealed that someone had been kneeling behind a roadside bush. Two spent cartridges were found on the ground. It looked like the Fountains had been ambushed.

The posse followed the tracks for about a hundred yards and found three sets of hoofprints, which had churned up the ground near the buckboard tracks. They also found evidence of men's boot prints. The boot prints were measured, and the posse took note of the hoofprints. Cigarette papers covered the ground; the horsemen had spent some time at this spot.

Sleet stopped the search for ten days, but when the posse returned to the spot, they found a puddle of blood by the roadside. It was splattered over a diameter of six feet. A blanket impression marked the sand by the blood, and nearby the posse discovered a blood-soaked handkerchief containing two powder-burned coins: a nickel and a dime.

That afternoon the buckboard was discovered twelve miles from Chalk Hill. Three sets of hoofprints and three sets of boot prints marked the area. Fountain's valise and boxes had been opened, and the contents were either strewn around or missing. Again they saw a blanket imprint on the ground. Something heavy had been laid on the blanket. The warning note that Fountain had received was found in the buckboard.

Five miles farther down the road, the posse found what looked like a campsite. Here horses had been fed, coffee and bacon had been cooked, and there was another print of a blanket with a heavy load on the ground. Footprints made by a child's shoe led away from the site for about six feet, but it was only the right shoe. The murderers were playing games with the law by creating a false trail.

The posse followed the trail east until it branched off into three directions. Here the posse split into three groups. Part of the posse followed the trail that headed west. Along this trail they found a grazing horse with a sore back, its side covered with dried, matted blood.

The second trail led northwest toward the Sacramento Mountains and Oliver Lee's Dog Canyon Ranch. When the posse was a few miles away from the ranch, they found that a herd of cattle had obliterated the trail with their own hoofprints. The third group of riders took the trail that led to the Jarillo Mountains and Lee's Wildy Well Ranch. Here they met Lee. They invited him to join them in the search, but he refused, adding, "What the hell are those sons of bitches to us?" When Lee rode away, his horse's hoofprints were examined and found to be the same as the ones the posse had followed.

With sensational banner headlines, newspapers all over the state covered the story of the missing Fountains. Governor Thornton was pressured to take some action. He decided that an outsider was needed, as the local sheriff's election was still being contested. He hired Pat Garrett, a former lawman who was best known for killing Billy the Kid and was now living in Texas as a private detective. Garrett, now poverty-stricken, thought that accepting this job would eventually lead to his appointment as sheriff and the $6,000 that came with it.

Thinking that a professional investigator was needed, the governor also hired the Pinkerton Agency. Pinkerton sent John C. Frazer, one of the agency's best operatives. Garrett felt he did not need the Pinkertons, and this attitude led to his less-than-complete cooperation with Frazer. As the investigation continued, Frazer reported to his home agency: "You can see how I have been handicapped in this matter and any information I have gotten from Garrett I have been compelled to draw out of him by asking question [sic] direct after having received information of what he possessed. I believe him thoroughly honest in his intentions, but may be a little careless and [he does] not consider certain points of much importance. I have been very careful not to let them know that I am aware of their having held information back from me and at the present time we are the very best of friends." Frazer was being kind. As time proved, Garrett was incompetent and was filled with too much self-importance.

Frazer continued with his investigation, constantly having to either reinvestigate what Garrett had already looked into or uncover new evidence that Garrett had set aside as unimportant. When Frazer's contract ran out, the Pinkertons sent another agent, but the damage to the case had already been done.

Garrett continued on the case and believed he had enough evidence to convict Oliver Lee and James Gililland. The case finally went to trial on June 13, 1899, more than three years after the disappearance of the Fountains. Thomas Catron was the prosecutor; Albert Fall was the defending attorney.

Catron decided to prosecute Lee and Gililland for the murder of Henry Fountain. He didn't think he had enough evidence to prosecute for the murder of Albert Fountain. McNew was still being held as one of the murderers of the father. He was held illegally and kept in jail for almost a year, but when no new evidence was uncovered, he was released. After his release, he worked as a ranger until his death in 1937.

Pat Garrett's case started unraveling. Witnesses either disappeared or changed their stories. Fall argued that anyone with size 7 boots could have made the imprints, and since no bodies were found, it could not be proved that the Fountains were dead; all that could be proved was that they were missing. It took the jury eight minutes to come back with a verdict of not guilty. All charges against Lee and Gililland were dropped.

Gililland spent the rest of his life ranching and traveling; he died in 1948. Lee and Fall spent their lives in politics; both changed their party affiliation from Democratic to Republican. Thomas Catron and Albert Fall were elected New Mexico's first U.S. senators. In 1921 Fall was appointed Secretary of the Interior by President Warren G. Harding, a position he resigned in 1923, when he was identified as the principal figure in the Tea Pot Dome scandal.

Thomas Catron has a county named after him; Oliver Lee, a memorial state park. Albert J. Fountain and his son Henry don't even have a grave. Their bodies were never found, and who killed them remains a mystery.

CHAPTER FIVE

The Secret of the School on the Hill

The temperature hovered around 30 degrees on this January 1943 morning, but that had no impact on the headmaster's decision to call a special outdoor meeting of the students. Immediately after breakfast, the forty-five students, all dressed in the required uniform of shorts and long-sleeved shirts, headed for seats outside of Fuller Lodge. The faculty was already seated there and waiting.

Some good-humored jostling took place, as is typical of schoolboys, but there was an overlay of curiosity and speculation. After all, it was just after the Christmas holidays and classes had just resumed, so what could be so important?

The headmaster stood in front of the lodge and made short work of his announcement. The school was closing. Classes would continue for the next few weeks, during which the whole year's curriculum would be covered. New Mexico state school tests would be administered before the middle of February, and the final day of school would be February 15.

That was the extent of the announcement. The students left more confused than they had been before they arrived. Why was the school closing? What would happen to their school? Would it be deserted? Would someone else take it over? What would become of it?

The parents were notified of the school's closing, but they could add little information to what the students already knew. The administration said only that the property had been sold to the government, and that the students and faculty were required to evacuate the land within weeks.

Yet before the end of January, even before the students completed their courses, their campus was invaded by strangers. The boys watched in awe as heavy construction equipment and workers arrived in what had been their isolated, idyllic domain. The students and faculty were gone by the middle of February, none the wiser of the future of their rugged school on the Pajarito Plateau of the Jemez Mountains, New Mexico.

This unique plateau, cut with canyons that formed fingers of land stretching east, was created and tempered by nature. With an altitude of more than 7,000 feet, separated by conical hills, some as high as 11,000 feet, the plateau is a rugged, challenging land. Its unique formation owes its characteristics to an extinct volcano. The plateau is a caldera, what was left when a blown volcano collapsed upon itself.

The isolated and inaccessible land attracted just a few settlers. Native Americans existed here off and on over the decades.

Old-time mountain men trapped for beaver in the Jemez streams. In the early 1900s a few farmers and a smattering of ranchers called the area home. In 1925 the Freys opened a guest ranch. The guests arrived by burros over a zigzagging narrow trail. But first they had to take a buckboard from Buckman, New Mexico, which was an outpost northwest of Santa Fe; cross the Rio Grande on a bridge that had a tendency to wash out; and then mount burros for the last heart-stopping part of the journey.

In 1918 Ashley Pond arrived and established his school. Pond's school soon became known for its high academic requirements and for its healthy lifestyle. The dress code of the boys-only student body was shorts and shirts, every day—all four seasons. Physical activity such as exploring the mountains on foot and on horseback was encouraged. The students slept on unheated porches but did have heated study rooms. It was a demanding school, and one for the rich, such as the son of a British consul, who was the first student enrolled.

Former students became titans of industry (in companies such as American Motors, Sears and Roebuck, and Quaker Oats); others achieved literary acclaim (Gore Vidal and William Burroughs); and some made their mark in other ways, such as Bill Veeck, the owner of the Chicago White Sox.

Given the school's outstanding academic reputation and the support of wealthy families, its closing was a puzzle—a puzzle that would not be solved for two years.

HARMON T. PARKHURST, COURTESY PALACE OF THE GOVERNORS PHOTO ARCHIVES (NMHM/DCA), #001238

The Los Alamos Ranch School prior to its closing.

Meanwhile, thirty-four miles away, a critical part of the mystery was taking place. At 109 East Palace, Santa Fe, in an old building surrounded by guards and fences, large numbers of men and women were seen coming and going.

Holding court inside the adobe was Dorothy McKibbin, a congenial woman in her forties. As friendly and pleasant as she was, she gave no indication as to her job, or the purpose of her office, to the curious. Yet, somehow, many felt that there was a connection between this small Santa Fe spot and the increase of traffic heading north.

The road north out of Santa Fe was a thrilling and challenging trip. It was a tortuous ride of unpaved, boulder-strewn, winding roads that snaked their way over mountain knobs and valleys, through volcanic fields, grasslands, and forests. Throughout its treacherous route, nature had blessed it with beautiful vistas. Now the ride was made tedious by up to five-hour waits as road crews dynamited the area, making improvements on the existing road, or in some spots building an entirely new road.

The citizens of Santa Fe figured that the destination of the many buses and old cars heading north must be the old school on the "hill." Some of these vehicles contained families, making the mystery even more compelling. The few whose curiosity and sense of adventure prodded them to follow the route to the former campus found the old school grounds gated and heavily guarded. Something big was going on.

Rumors were flying. It seemed to be some sort of military compound. Some wondered whether gas warfare research was being conducted on the site. Others speculated that rockets, jet propulsion, or death rays were being developed. There was some humorous speculation that they were manufacturing windshield wipers for submarines. But perhaps the most ludicrous notion was that the old school had become a Republican internment camp.

The "hill" employed local and out-of-state people. Native American women were hired on as maids for the families living at the old school. They reported for work dressed in their colorful Pueblo clothes—bright belted mantas, high deerskin boots, beautiful shawls covering their shoulders and head—and adorned with an abundance of turquoise jewelry. They added a colorful and unusual touch to the otherwise drab military look of the campus.

The old school property took on an international sound and look as Hispanics, Native Americans, and people from all over the country came to work in this small town. Some of the employees heard about jobs from friends and relatives and came from other states. They found plenty of available jobs for unskilled and semiskilled workers. The country was at war, and working men were at a premium. But men were not the only employees sought. Women found work as secretaries, clerks, and teachers for the elementary, middle, and high schools that had been established there.

Those employees brought stories of the lifestyle of the compound's residents to the outside world. Those who lived there seemed to be leading very normal lives, with tots playing on swing sets, young students traveling in laughing groups to and from school, wives going to the grocery store, and laundry hanging in backyards. People in Socorro, Santa Fe, and other surrounding New Mexico towns heard about the quickly constructed two-story apartments, the family hutments (small houses), and the prefabricated units. They heard about the commissary and the library. But they heard nothing about the work being conducted. On the way to their jobs, the outside employees passed gate after gate, heavily guarded by military police, all located away from their destination, which was the public areas.

For all the look of a small rural town, the "hill" was still a secret installation. Mail did not arrive directly but was routed through Santa Fe. All communication was controlled; outgoing mail was censored, and phone calls were monitored. "Hill" residents knew that hidden eyes watched their every move when they left the compound. And there were no dinnertime conversations about how one's day went.

The locals employed at the site could shed no light on the true purpose of the "hill." They did their specific jobs, providing services to the ramshackle town that had grown up overnight, but they never got near the secret areas. All that was evident was the tight security, the increased traffic, and the military look of the compound.

Over the next two years, the parade of trucks, buses, and autos heading for the "hill" became routine, and citizens in the area became preoccupied with their wartime lives, gradually accepting the mystery on the hill.

Although security was tight, leaks did occur. As the "hill" expanded its operations, aircraft were used to keep in touch with happenings. Communication was via shortwave radio. Unfortunately, the wavelength that was used posed some problems. The employees of a railroad freight yard in San Antonio, Texas, were perplexed when their communications were constantly interrupted with mysterious messages as they shifted their railcars.

The community center in Los Alamos, New Mexico,
after the Los Alamos Ranch School's closing in 1943.

You didn't need to be in Texas to hear these messages. Listeners to the Voice of America were thoroughly confused, and frustrated, as these strange conversations continually cut into their programs.

Again construction equipment and crews were seen in the vicinity, not heading for the "hill" in the north, but south, closer to the town of San Antonio. Why anyone would want to do any building there was a puzzle. That land, called Jornada del Muerto (Journey of the Dead Man), was about as useless as a piece of land could be, lacking water and any significant plant growth.

There was so little life in this area that it was used by Alamogordo Air Base as a training bombing site for crews who would soon head for the European and Pacific war zones. The locals concluded that the construction activity had something to do with the practice bombings.

By midsummer in 1944 the number of trucks passing through Santa Fe heading north increased. The residents in the area had become so used to the traffic going in that direction that few noticed the change. Even the constant stream of other vehicles from the "hill" heading south drew little interest.

Some people in Albuquerque suspected that something was going on up north, but they paid little attention to the increase in traffic. Since few of these vehicles stopped in Albuquerque, their passing through was hardly noticed. However, a small restaurant called Roys in Belan saw a great increase in its luncheon crowd. Another popular stop for these evasive caravans was Miera's bar in San Antonio. Where these drivers were headed, and why, was still a secret. No one could imagine why so many people were driving around in this remote, fairly unpopulated area.

By May 1945 the war in Europe was in its last days. On May 7 just before dawn, residents around the Alamogordo bombing site saw a large orange ball in the sky, indicating that a huge amount of TNT had been detonated. Some thought the army had exploded some excess artillery. There was little reason to connect it with happenings in any other part of the state. In reality, it was part of the secret on the "hill," a test of sorts.

In the last weeks of June 1945, those roaming the streets in Santa Fe at night could spot trucks coming from the direction of the old school and heading south. Sometimes the convoys were small, with as few as two trucks. At other times convoys of ten or so trucks would rumble their way through the town.

It was not just the ranchers who were concerned about the weather on July 15. Summer thunder showers had swept in, and while most people were happy to get the rain, the nervous personnel on the "hill" were not. They watched the sky and checked charts repeatedly. At 7:45 p.m. on July 15, 1945, four vehicles made their way out of the "hill" compound. The three army sedans, followed by a GI truck, stopped briefly on the Santa Fe road and then continued on in the direction of Albuquerque. On the outskirts of the city, the small convoy pulled off to the side of the road. After the occupants conferred, the vehicles were regrouped and continued into the city, where they refueled at Wilson's garage.

After filling up the gas tanks, the vehicles seemed to wander around town for about forty-five minutes making random stops, one of which was the Hilton, where more passengers were picked up. The convoy then headed south out of the city. Passing through San Antonio, the vehicles turned off the main road and headed for a group of bivouacked military men. After a brief stop, the cars and the truck proceeded to a military police post. The caravan had reached its destination. The passengers in the car set about making themselves comfortable on blankets scattered about the ground.

Other observers at the site hunkered down in shelters, built of wood with walls of reinforced concrete buried under huge layers of earth. These shelters were spaced 20,000 feet apart and were situated around the area facing north, west, and south.

At 5:00 a.m., fourteen miles away from the observers, searchlights began dancing around the sky. The private radio communication system came to life at 5:20 a.m., announcing that the event would take place in about ten minutes.

The observers at the site were not the only ones watching the night sky. Word of something big about to take place was buzzing around the old school, and daily workers had taken their observations and speculation back to Santa Fe and Socorro. Even Mrs. McKibbin was urged to rise very early and watch the sky for something spectacular.

In San Antonio, Jose Miera was awakened from a sound sleep and told to come outside to see something "the world had never seen before." Outside San Antonio, some residents of the "hill" waited in their sleeping bags, eyes on the sky. Others at the "hill" knew something big was going to happen, and they waited on their porches in the black of night, their attention focused skyward.

For miles around the area, eyes constantly scanned the sky, looking for they knew not what. As the predawn hours went by, nothing happened. Only blackness greeted the viewers. Shortly after 5:00 a.m. a local radio station signed on the air with Tchaikovsky's *Nutcracker Suite,* which was strangely mixed with a countdown. At 5:29 a.m. on July 16, 1945, a strange sun rose in the south.

An intense light appeared, brighter than the sun had ever been. The intensity diminished, but the light was still brilliant as it turned first to yellow, then to red, then to purple. A ball of fire ascended, followed by a column of white smoke topped by a mushroom-shaped cloud.

Nearly two minutes after the flash of light came the shock wave. It bounced off the surrounding mountains like thunder. The shock wave broke windows 120 miles away and was felt as far away as 160 miles.

An observer described what he saw: First he saw an intense flash of light and then felt a sensation of heat on all his exposed body parts. He had the impression that "suddenly the country-side became brighter than in full daylight. A conglomeration of flames promptly started rising. After a few seconds the rising flames lost their brightness and appeared as a huge pillar of smoke with an expanded head like a gigantic mushroom that rose rapidly beyond the clouds."

Another eyewitness thought it was "awe-inspiring." It "did not fit into any preconception possessed by anybody. The most startling feature was the intense light."

Not all who saw the phenomenon were favorably impressed. One military man remarked, "The long-hairs have let it get away from them!"

It didn't take the men long to finish their work on the site after the explosion. They loaded up and headed back to their school on the "hill," Los Alamos. They were an ambivalent group filled not only with triumph for their scientific achievement but also with terror for what they had unleashed.

In early August 1945 President Harry S. Truman announced that the United States had developed an atomic bomb. The secret of the school on the "hill" was out. Finally, everything made sense to the people around Santa Fe, San Antonio, and other towns who had watched the heavy traffic going north and south, the building of new roads in that direction, the increase in the number of strangers around town, the heavy security, and the shroud of silence that covered the area.

Of all the news coverage, political reports, comments, and general talk, the most insightful—and prophetic—statement came from the man who was in charge of the "secret." Quoting from an ancient Hindu scripture, the physicist J. Robert Oppenheimer remarked, "Now I am become Death, the destroyer of worlds."

CHAPTER SIX

The Curious Cowboy and the Mysterious Bones

To friends and neighbors George McJunkin was an honorable man, a curious, intelligent, and kind man. To strangers he was a black cowboy. That didn't bother McJunkin; he had other things to wonder about, such as the characteristics of the various rocks he found, and the names and uses of the many plants he saw, and how to tell time by the stars.

Some might call McJunkin an uneducated man. He had no formal schooling, yet he taught himself to read and write. Later in life he learned to use a transit for laying straight lines, and with it he laid out the barbed-wire fencing on his ranch. From a soldier he learned how to use a telescope, and armed with books, he studied the stars.

He was born a slave in Texas. During the Civil War, a troop of Union soldiers rode onto the ranch where he and his father lived, declared that all slaves were free, and rode off again.

McJunkin was curious about what lay beyond the Texas ranch. He wanted to be truly free. When he was fourteen, he left home, taking with him a knowledge of blacksmithing, which he had learned from his father, and the ability to ride and rope, which he had learned from some Mexican neighbors.

McJunkin headed north via the cattle trails, where he took a series of jobs with outfits on the drives. He made friends, perfected his bronco-busting and roping skills, and earned his position as foreman of Bob Jack's Crowfoot Ranch near Folsom, New Mexico.

On occasion he would face the prejudice of the time. Once, when enjoying a meal in a Folsom cafe, a couple of newcomers loudly made it known that they would not eat with a black man. He would have to go. McJunkin went to eat in the kitchen and was joined by every customer in the cafe. The newcomers soon learned who was respected in town and who was unwanted.

McJunkin was very well respected—by his cowboys, by his neighbors, and always by his employers. While he was well liked by the Anglos, he especially enjoyed the company of his Mexican friends. From them he learned how to play the guitar and the violin, and with those skills he livened up many a party.

He was considered one of the best broncobusters and ropers in New Mexico. But for all of that McJunkin still liked to ride the fence line and learn from nature. He was forever picking up strange plants, rocks, or old bones and showing them to his neighbors. Some were identified for him by Chicanos whose families had lived in the West for generations. He would put these special finds on his mantelpiece. On one ride he discovered what looked like a very old skull. This too went on the mantel-piece. They were his treasure trove, his special museum.

Never did he suspect that this treasure trove would shake the archaeological world or change the thinking of the world's scientists. And it all started with a sudden, violent storm.

On August 27, 1908, huge black clouds began gathering over Johnson Mesa near Folsom, New Mexico. A cloudburst was coming, and a bad one at that. Seeing what Mother Nature had in store, McJunkin hurried to the ranch house, cranked up the phone, and tried to raise Mrs. Rooke, the telephone operator, so that she could warn the ranchers of the impending storm. He tried several times to contact her, but she never answered.

By this time, the day was darker than night, and the clouds poured huge raindrops on roofs and the ground. Any cattle near the river were sure to be drowned, especially if the dam broke. McJunkin threw on his slicker and went out into the rain to check the dam. As the rain made gullies around the structure, it was barely holding. A later check showed that the rain had done its work: The dam was gone, the water was halfway up to his boot tops, and under it was a layer of slippery mud. Trees were down and were traveling around the land, propelled by the wind and rain, and a great surge of water was coming down the valley.

The rain finally stopped the next morning, and McJunkin went out to inspect the damage and check on his neighbors. The bridge had washed out, and half the houses in the town of Folsom were under water. The streets were covered with a running stream about four feet deep. The search started for the missing townspeople, and by the end of the day the count was up to fifteen. Mrs. Rooke was never found. Her house had washed away. Because she stayed at her post calling the ranchers and townspeople, warning them of the dangerous weather, it was too late for her to seek safety.

Before the storm Folsom had been a big cattle town in competition with the cattle towns in Texas. But the rain changed that. Never again would Folsom be considered a cow town. The rain took more than Folsom's neighbors; it took its livelihood, and its heart.

The fifty-seven-year-old McJunkin needed to check his land, and age was slowing him down. He took one of his younger cowhands with him as he went on the inspection ride. They rode along Wild Horse Arroyo, which before the storm had been about two or three feet deep. A wide chasm more than ten feet deep now greeted them. The fence that once crossed the arroyo hung partially suspended in space and presented a danger to cattle.

Studying the damage, McJunkin's eyes traveled down to the bottom of the arroyo. Then something caught his eye. Sticking out of the bank, near the bottom, was something white. His natural curiosity drove him down to have a look.

When he got to the bottom, he spotted a large white bone partially stuck in the bank. It was about ten feet below the top. Around it were several smaller bones. Using barbed-wire clippers,

McJunkin carefully cleared the dirt away from the big object. He thought it was the biggest buffalo bone he had ever seen. This bone would be an interesting addition to his treasure trove.

After that find, every time he rode by the arroyo on his ranch rounds, he would think about the bones there. He called the spot the Bone Pit because there were so many of them in various sizes implanted in that bank. He wondered how they got there and what kind of bones they were, for they were nothing like the cattle, buffalo, and wildlife bones he had seen. It was a mystery that was always on his mind. He talked about the bones to a few people in Folsom. No one had an answer, and most of the cowboys showed no interest. However, he did hear about a man in Las Vegas, New Mexico, who knew about old bones, so McJunkin wrote him a letter. The man never came to look, and nothing came of this correspondence.

In 1912 McJunkin was on his way to Raton, New Mexico, when an iron tire on his wagon came loose. He took the wagon to a blacksmith in town for repairs. Outside the shop the blacksmith, Carl Schwachheim, had a fancy fountain decorated with two huge sets of interlocking elk antlers. That prompted a conversation about big animal bones, and McJunkin told Schwachheim of the bones he had found. He described the location and invited the blacksmith to have a look. Schwachheim was also a collector of nature and was anxious to see the Bone Pit, but he was too busy to take the trip. Besides, he didn't have a horse or an automobile, so he had no way to get out to the bone site.

A few years went by, and no one came up with any answers, but McJunkin's interest in the bones had grown instead of diminishing. In a conversation with Fred Howarth, who worked at the Raton bank in New Mexico, McJunkin mentioned his bones. Howarth too collected oddities of nature. He thought that someday he would like to see the Bone Pit. McJunkin gave him directions just in case he could make the trip.

Some time later, when the Crowfoot Ranch cattle were grazing at Stuyvesant Springs Ranch near the Capulin Mountains, McJunkin was staying in a small log cabin he used while he worked the range. To make the cabin more comfortable, McJunkin brought some of his treasures from the mantel at his Crowfoot Ranch house. One day a horrendous storm hit the area, and while it wasn't as severe as the Folsom flood storm, a lightning bolt did hit the roof of the log cabin and started a fire. McJunkin was now an old man, and his aching body was no match for the fire. He tried carrying buckets of water to throw on the flaming cabin, but he was too slow, and the cabin burned to the ground. Unfortunately, his prized possessions—the Indian skull and the big bones—could not be saved. All were destroyed in the fire.

McJunkin no longer had the strength to do the demanding ranch work. Bob Jack, the owner, had recently died, and his wife offered to sell McJunkin the ranch, but he was now too old. He moved into a hotel in Folsom and spent his last days in a small room visited by his many friends and tended by the town doctor.

McJunkin's days came to an end on July 1, 1922. He died never knowing that he had found the first clue to the mystery that had been swirling around the anthropology world for decades. When did humans come to America? The mystery probably would have gone on for several more years or perhaps even decades, if it wasn't for the curiosity McJunkin sparked in Schwachheim and Howarth and, through them, in the scientific world as well.

Shortly after McJunkin's death, Schwachheim and Howarth found they had some free time. They formed a small expedition to the Bone Pit, accompanied by several other interested parties from the Raton area. They were able to gather several specimens from the pit and take them back to Raton, where they laid the bones out to study. Using several reference books, they came to the conclusion that none of them had any idea what the bones represented.

In January 1926, eighteen years after McJunkin's discovery, Howarth and Schwachheim went to Denver on business. While there they contacted J. D. Figgins, head of the Colorado Museum of Natural History. They brought their bones with them. Figgins immediately recognized the uniqueness of the bones and believed that the Bone Pit might be an important find. In March of that year, Figgins and another scientist traveled to the Crowfoot Ranch to see the Bone Pit for themselves. What they discovered was an area with many bones of a type never seen before. They were the bones of an extinct species.

The Bone Pit created new questions concerning not only the species but also the age of the bones, and how the extinct animals had died. Figgins was able to mount a major excavation project of this pit in 1927. This and other future excavations in the area revealed an astonishing discovery and answered some of the questions that had been plaguing the studies of America's early humans. In between the fossilized ribs of what was an ancient species of bison, they found a flint point. That animal had been killed—by a human.

The Folsom bison bones with the Folsom point.

As is typical of science, when one question is answered, other questions arise. If the bison had been killed by a human, where had this person come from, and when did the kill occur?

At the time when George McJunkin was digging up his big bones, the scientific community was in an uneasy agreement that humans did not appear in America until about 4,000 years ago, although not everyone in the field of archaeology supported this hypothesis. However, there was no proof to refute it, so science worked with that assumed date.

Then along came McJunkin's big bones. Through carbon dating, the approximate age of the bones was established. The human and the bison had their confrontation more than 10,000 years ago. The killing point embedded in the bison's ribs was proof that the hypothesis that humans came to America 4,000 years ago was incorrect.

While the point found in the bison's rib cage proved that the animal had been killed by a human, and the other bones found on this site pointed to several killings, the area showed little evidence that it was a major butchering site or that humans had established a camp or living site there. No tools made from bone or stone were found in the area, and evidence of hides was rare. That means that the major work on the kill was performed elsewhere.

This led to a series of questions on why humans were in this area. Was this site on a migration route, and was the kill made only to feed people as they traveled somewhere else? Where were they going, and why?

As it turned out later, further archaeological excavations about fifty miles south of Folsom showed that the Folsom human was not the earliest human to walk and hunt in America.

Rigely Whiteman, a young Native American, discovered another ancient killing site in the Blackwater Draw near Clovis.

Most of the excavations there took place between 1936 and 1938. These excavations uncovered a pre-Folsom culture complex that was named "Clovis," after the nearest town. It proved to be an older culture, dating back between 13,000 and 12,200 years ago, and it is classified as a prehistoric Paleo-Indian culture site. During that particular time, Blackwater Draw was a marshy land of seasonal ponds and would have made an ideal gathering and feeding place for bison and mammoths. The abundance of these large animals made it a perfect place for prehistoric humans to hunt. This Clovis culture is estimated to have lasted from 200 to 800 years, starting about 13,000 years ago. The Folsom culture followed.

What distinguishes the Clovis from the Folsom culture, in addition to the carbon dating, is the style of the points found. The Folsom points are more finely worked than the Clovis points and show chip marks over their whole surface.

However, the Clovis site produced more in the way of artifacts and included two long bone points with impact damage, stone blades, a part of a Clovis blade core, and several cutting tools made of stone. The Clovis site looked more like an inhabited site, or at least a working site, than did the Folsom site. Over the years further excavations uncovered Clovis culture sites throughout the United States and even in Central America and South America.

Although Folsom sites are fewer, McJunkin's Folsom site does not stand alone. Dozens of other Folsom sites have been found throughout America. But McJunkin's find does represent the first discovered proof of humans arriving in America thousands of years ago. Because of the Folsom discovery, scientists changed their way of thinking and were prompted to search for other sites, thus uncovering an earlier culture, the Clovis.

Together these and other sites have caused speculation and theorizing. Does the route show the advancement of technology from north to south, or does the advanced technology indicate the migration route that humans took, arriving in the south and traveling north to Canada?

Could the Folsom hunters be actual descendants of the earlier Clovis humans? Or were they another migratory group, totally unrelated? If they were descendants, why did they leave the earlier site and move farther north?

Some researchers believe that since the findings at Clovis were so extensive, the area could have been hunted out, or weather changes could have forced the migration of the game and the people who followed their food.

While Folsom and Clovis sites show that humans were in America as early as 13,000 years ago, the evidence doesn't tell us where they came from. Some researchers theorize that humans came across a frozen Bering Sea from Siberia. The earlier Clovis site, south of Folsom, may mean that humans came up from the south, making the crossing over a frozen Atlantic from France. Prehistoric sites in France have produced points remarkably similar to the Clovis points, with their face flaked on both edges alternately with a percussor.

Is the mystery of early humans' arrival in America as easy as that? Could humans have arrived from the north or the south and slowly migrated in the opposite direction, establishing a culture as they moved and leaving signs of it in the land? And if that answers the question of where Clovis and Folsom humans came from, where did they go? And when?

Do the Native American cultures in America today have their roots deep in Clovis and Folsom humans? Were the residents of Chaco Canyon the descendants of these prehistoric humans? If so, the link to these 10,000- to 13,000-year-old cultures is still undiscovered.

Or did early humans in America die off because their food source disappeared? According to some researchers, a climate change in the form of a cold phase killed off the large animals that Clovis and Folsom humans hunted. Others insist that a large comet caused the mass extinction. Research conducted in 2009 claims that there was no extraterrestrial impact, but that doesn't explain why metal and magnetic bits were found inside the bones of ancient mammoths.

All of these scientific theories and discoveries began with George McJunkin, whose innate curiosity and ability to observe nature led him to the Bone Pit. His sharing of the mysterious bones with others is what prompted the work in New Mexico at the Folsom site. If not for George McJunkin, we might still think that Columbus and the Native Americans arrived in America at the same time.

CHAPTER SEVEN

The Treasure of Victorio Peak

It started with a deer-hunting trip and turned into a fiasco that included the U.S. Army, attorney F. Lee Bailey, the grandson of Jesse James, the state of New Mexico, the Apache chief Victorio, Emperor Maximilian, and assorted men and women who were lusting after a fortune in gold. The debacle came about all because of an ambitious and reckless man who didn't want to get wet.

Milton Ernest "Doc" Noss and his wife, Ova, whom he called "Babe," had quite a few friends in Hot Springs (present-day Truth or Consequences, New Mexico). Doc was the local chiropodist.

Doc got by because he was tall, handsome, and a charmer. Babe wasn't much to look at, but she had an enthusiastic personality, and her outspoken nature defined her as a character. Either you liked Babe, and many did, or you avoided her. It was these characteristics that were to sustain her in her lifelong battle with the people, including officials at government agencies, who tried to take her legacy away, a legacy that was discovered on a misty, rainy day in November 1937.

On that day Doc, Babe, and four friends headed out from Hot Springs for a deer-hunting trip. They camped by a small stream in the Hembrillo Basin near Victorio Peak. The peak was named after the Apache chief Victorio, who had torn up the area with his avenging raids on all who entered the territory.

Doc was a loner and soon left the other hunters to make his own way. As he hunted at the base of the mountain, which was really a large hill of five hundred feet, it began to sprinkle. He looked around for shelter, but the area was barren of trees or any brush that could keep him dry. So he decided to climb up the mountain, when he spotted a large boulder near the top. Figuring it was better than nothing, he sought refuge in what shelter it could give him.

While he was standing there, he noticed that the area showed signs of having been worked by humans. At his feet he spied a rock with some man-made signs on it. He bent to pick up the rock, which turned out to be heavier than it looked. Struggling, he hefted the rock. Pushing it aside, he saw that it covered a shaft that disappeared down into the mountain.

It all looked very mysterious to Doc. Peering into the dark, he noticed a wooden pole with intermittent notches leaning against one wall of the shaft. Doc couldn't wait to get back to Babe and tell her of his find. He had already decided that the discovery of the shaft was his and Babe's secret.

A few weeks after the hunting trip, Doc and Babe returned to Victorio Peak with equipment for exploring the shaft. Doc removed the rock covering the shaft. Using a rope to climb down, instead of trusting the rotting pole ladder, he maneuvered his way cautiously down the narrow slit and past a large boulder hanging from the ceiling that partially blocked his way. Babe stood outside the shaft watching his progress. Doc had secured the rope around Babe's ankle, and they had worked out a series of signals based on tugs on the rope.

The shaft ended in a small room. His miner's lamp illuminated what looked like ancient Indian drawings on the walls of the tiny chamber. Some of these looked painted and still showed some trace of color, while others had been chiseled into the rock.

At one end of this small chamber, the shaft continued, sloping downward. This shaft descended about 120 feet and came to an end in a large natural cavern.

It was here that Doc made a gruesome discovery. Scattered around the room were skeletons, all in a kneeling position pegged to the ground with their hands tied behind their backs. In an adjoining alcove he discovered what looked like a burial chamber stacked with more skeletons. Some of these bones were scattered, but by counting skulls he came up with a total of seventy-nine skeletons.

He saw several smaller rooms chiseled out of the rock along one wall. As he explored these rooms, he found riches of untold wealth—jewels, coins, saddles, and priceless artifacts like jeweled swords, crowns of gold, and golden religious statues. He also saw a Wells Fargo box and leather pouches stacked to the ceiling. Lying around were quite a few papers, including letters, the latest of which was dated 1880. In one of the side rooms, he saw pig iron bars piled chest high like cords of wood.

He filled his pockets with gold coins, grabbed a jeweled dagger, and made his way back up the narrow passages to Babe. The dagger was a work of ancient art. Its scabbard was fashioned from a piece of metal encrusted with rubies and emeralds that had been carved into figures by a long-forgotten craftsman. He couldn't wait to show Babe the dagger and tell her of the treasure that lay under the mountain. He mentioned the room filled with pig iron bars because it was so incongruous compared with the golden artifacts and coins. Babe insisted he go back to get a bar.

Again Doc descended the narrow passages, squeezed through to the large chamber, found the room with the pig iron, and sorted through the pile until he found one he thought he could carry.

On the way back he struggled with the cigar-shaped bar, which despite its size was quite heavy, making the difficult trip even more hazardous. As he made his way back up, the bar scraped along the walls of the narrow passage. When he reached Babe, he showed her the black bar, informing her that she had to be content with this bar because he was not going to bring any more up. She took it and turned it over, discovering that part of the blackened exterior had scraped off and what was underneath was gleaming yellow—gold. Stunned at what they saw, Doc said, "If it's gold, and all that other is gold like it, we can call John D. Rockefeller a tramp."

From that time on, Doc and Babe spent every spare moment exploring the tunnels and working the claim. They stayed in a tent at the base of Victorio Peak. Doc did some simple math and figured that the bars were worth several million dollars. Every time Doc went into the mountain, he brought out two gold bars and some artifacts. Each time, Babe stood guard at the top, nervously waiting for him to appear from the depths of the mountain.

This huge treasure trove had its effect on Doc. He became paranoid, suspecting everyone and trusting no one, not even his wife. After a day in the mountain, he would disappear into the desert at night, secretly burying pieces of his treasure and telling no one its location.

Although the gold bars alone would have made him an exceedingly rich man, they did Doc very little good. Four years before his discovery, Congress had passed the Gold Act, which prohibited private citizens from owning gold.

Of course, there was a black market in gold. But huge amounts could not be sold at one time without drawing suspicion to him and increasing the chances that someone might find the source of the bars. Doc needed to be very careful in determining how many bars he sold and to whom he sold them. He knew that dealing with the black market would mean dealing with unscrupulous and dangerous individuals. Doc continued "mining" the treasures of the peak, hiding much of it in the desert.

In the spring of 1938, he and Babe went to Santa Fe and filed a lease for the section of land surrounding Victorio Peak, the mining rights on and around the peak, and, most importantly, a treasure trove claim. Now that he had legal claim to the land, Doc conducted an open operation. However, his paranoia did not lessen, and he would steal off in the night to bury his treasure in the desert. Doc had certain landmarks. Sometimes he dug near a road; sometimes the treasure went into a rancher's stock tank or some other identifiable area. Only Doc knew where the loot was.

In the fall of 1938, Doc decided to enlarge the passageway by blasting away the huge boulder that partially blocked one of the shafts. He employed S. E. Montgomery, a mining engineer, to do the blasting. Doc and Montgomery argued about the amount of dynamite needed, and Montgomery won out. The eight sticks of dynamite he used caused a cave-in, which blocked off the passage to the large room with tons of debris. Doc could no longer reach his trove.

Doc tried many times to dig his way through the debris and into the cavern, but he was unsuccessful. He became frustrated and angry, taking out his disappointment on his wife Babe. Now, instead of thousands of gold bars, he had only the few hundred bars he had buried in the desert.

The relationship between Babe and Doc deteriorated, and they eventually separated. Apparently Doc attempted to divorce Babe, but the papers were never served. Two years later, despite his still legitimate marriage to Babe, Doc married Violet Lena Boles, an act that would complicate the ownership of the treasure.

In 1946 Doc's legal claim to the mountain was running out. Babe went to Santa Fe to renew the claim, but the authorities insisted they could not renew it in Doc's name unless he made the request in person. However, they informed Babe, they could renew it in her name. With no other way to ensure legal possession of the treasure trove and the mining rights, Babe finally agreed.

In 1949 Doc met miner Charley Ryan, who convinced him that he could reopen the shaft. Doc agreed to a deal in which he would pay Ryan $25,000 to do just that. But access to Victorio Peak was denied. Since the claim was now filed in Babe's name, access to the area was denied to both of them until the official ownership could be determined.

Believing that Ryan would double-cross him, Doc made arrangements with an acquaintance, Tony Jolly, to relocate his gold. On the night of March 4, 1949, the two dug up and reburied 110 bars of gold. The next day, suspecting that Doc was trying to cut him out of the deal, Ryan accosted Doc. They got into a heated argument, and Ryan pulled out a gun. Doc headed for his pickup. Thinking Doc was going for his rifle, Ryan shot Doc, hitting him in the head and killing him. Twelve years after he had discovered his treasure, the man who potentially had millions lay dying in the dust with $2.16 in his pocket. Ryan was charged with murder, but since it seemed to be an act of self-defense, he was acquitted.

With Doc now gone, Babe could turn her attention to the peak. For the next six years, she occasionally hired men to work at clearing the shaft. The progress was slow, but Babe could only do what she could afford, and that wasn't much.

In 1955 the military expanded its operations at the White Sands Missile Base and included Victorio Peak in its domain. They forbade anyone except official personnel entrance to the area. Babe continued to fight for access to her gold mountain. She wrote letters appealing to state senators and to army generals.

By 1958 the story of Babe and Doc's gold was relegated to the status of myth. No one believed Babe and her fable of riches in Victorio Peak. Then in 1961 a couple of air force men changed everything and added to the mystery and the fight.

Airman First Class Thomas Berlett and Captain Leonard V. Fiege from Holloman Air Force Base went exploring and discovered a fissure in the mountain, which they said led to a cavern filled with gold bars. Wanting to keep their find a secret, they filled the fissure with dirt and rubble. Knowing they were on military property, the men decided it was prudent to let the army know what they had found.

After receiving Fiege and Berlett's report, the army decided to take action. Three officers, including Captain Fiege, were ordered to work the claim on the advice of the director of the Mint. The men, accompanied by government officials, including a secret service agent and fourteen military policemen, returned to the mountain on August 5, 1961. However, they were unable to penetrate the fissure beyond the rubble area. The military then began a full-scale mining operation.

In October of that year, Babe heard rumors that the military was conducting a mining operation at Victorio Peak. She contacted the New Mexico State Land Office and informed officials of her suspicions. State officials notified the army that they had leased only the top of the land to the military. The state of New Mexico claimed that everything underground, including the mineral rights, belonged to the state and other legal license holders. The military was ordered to stop operations, and in December 1961 the mining operation was shut down.

A search of legal documents in New Mexico produced the claims of Doc and Babe. As it turned out, the state of New Mexico did not exactly own the land. When the state had been initially laid out, every sixteenth section in a township was set aside by New Mexico for a school. The Noss claims were on Section 16. Yet a man by the name of Roy Henderson had leased it to the army. A compromise of sorts was worked out. The army could use only the surface, but no one was allowed on the property without the army's permission.

Shortly after that, the Gladdis Mining Company, working with the Denver Mint and the Museum of New Mexico, received permission to carry out an archaeological survey of the area. They were given three months to complete the survey. On June 20, 1963, they began operations, mapping the peak, moving tons of earth, and drilling a number of small test holes. This operation cost the government $250,000 and produced neither treasure nor any hint of one.

By 1972 word of the treasure at Victorio Peak was public knowledge, thanks to media coverage of the various diggings. Attorney F. Lee Bailey entered into the fray. He was representing fifty clients who felt they had a claim in the treasure, if there was a treasure. It was later learned that these clients included former White Sands Missile Site employees.

The missile site employees were not the only ones claiming ownership of the fortune. By right of her supposed marriage to the deceased Doc, Violet Noss Young, Doc's second wife, registered her ownership of the mountain. Jesse James III said that the treasure was his grandfather's hidden loot and therefore was his. The military men who had "discovered" the fissure into the room with gold bars put in their claim. Fiege and seven others formed a corporation called "Seven Heirs," claiming a right to the treasure based on their discovery through the fissure. And, of course, Babe Noss was still staking her claim.

A Florida group called Expedition Unlimited claimed the right to work the mountain. The members of this group based this claim on the fact that they were a professional treasure-hunting organization that had experience and would use scientific means.

In 1977 the overwhelmed military finally granted Expedition Unlimited the contract, with the understanding that they were representing all the other claimants and that the work must be completed in two weeks. Using the latest scientific procedures and equipment, Expedition Unlimited attacked the mountain. After two weeks they came up with nothing.

In 1979 Babe died, fighting until the end for her right to the treasure. Her grandson, Terry Delonas, who grew up on stories of the Victorio Peak treasure, formed a company called the Ova Noss Family Partnership (ONFP) and took up the fight. By selling shares in the company, he was able to raise enough money to proceed with extensive testing and excavation of the mountain.

Eventually it took a special act of Congress in 1989 to allow Delonas and the ONFP to work the site. Over a period of several years, the ONFP hired scientists to take readings of the mountain with sophisticated equipment; then the partnership moved in mining experts who used powerful equipment to search for shafts and fissures. Tunnels to facilitate exploration were constructed. This expedition was able to prove that there were old shafts and natural caverns in the mountain, but it produced no treasure.

Rumors swirled around saying that a treasure had never existed, that it was only in Doc's imagination. Delonas set about proving the doubters wrong. He was able to locate and interview twenty people who had seen proof of the treasure.

Today, the Noss family reportedly has a few old artifacts, although many were stolen from them, including a gold crown, pictures, and some old papers taken from the treasure cache.

Tony Jolly also bears testimony to Doc's treasure; he swears that he saw at least 110 gold bars the night he helped Doc dig up and rebury the gold. Eventually Jolly was able to dig up twenty of the bars. Ten were stolen from him, but with the other ten he managed to live a very comfortable life.

The mystery remains. Is there a treasure in the mountain? And if there is or was a treasure in Victorio Peak, who put it there? Since Doc claimed that he saw a letter dated 1880, some of it had to be deposited before the twentieth century. Also, the reported variety of objects, representing assorted cultures and societies, would indicate that it was not just one group that had buried its wealth, although it could have been one group that had buried the wealth of many other cultures. Were the caverns and rooms of Victorio Peak more a depository for a number of different people over the years? Was the treasure put there by a combination of robbers, religious figures, and vengeful bands?

Chief Victorio is an excellent candidate for being the originator, or at least a contributor, of this treasure. This was his territory. He raided, captured, and attacked churches, stagecoaches, trains, riders, and settlements, taking not only prisoners but any and all wealth he could find. He knew that whites honored gold, and he was determined to deprive them of their gold. That certainly would explain the diversity of the collection. It would also explain the skeletons.

Some researchers even credit this treasure trove to Emperor Maximilian of Mexico, whose vast wealth disappeared in the 1860s. Nonetheless, how it would wind up 2,000 miles away from Mexico City is a puzzle.

Padre La Rue could also have been the originator of the treasure. He was a poor priest who volunteered to travel to the New World in the eighteenth century to work with the poor. He reigned over the farmers on a large Mexican hacienda, but when the crops failed and the people were faced with starvation, he moved the village north. An old man that La Rue was caring for at the hacienda told him the story of a lush basin with good water and a mountain with a rich gold vein located north of El Paso.

Some people believe that Padre La Rue found this mountain of gold, and it was Victorio Peak, which was then called Soledad. According to legend, La Rue and his peasants worked the rich gold vein they found, turning the ore into primitive gold bars. When officials of the Spanish government went looking for La Rue, they found that the original hacienda had been abandoned. They sent an army out to search for him. Learning of the approaching army, La Rue hid the entrances to his gold mountain. He was captured and tortured, but he never revealed his secret. That would explain the primitive gold bars, but not the other items, especially the letters and the Wells Fargo chest.

The Noss family believes in the treasure. They also believe that gold was removed from the mountain. They are convinced that the U.S. government found a way into the mountain and its treasure. The army's position is cautious. No one in the army has ever admitted to seeing or removing any gold from the mountain.

Since no one has been able to reach the large cavern with its small side room of gold bars, nothing can be proven. For all anyone knows, the gold and artifacts could still be there, guarded by the skeletons.

CHAPTER EIGHT

The Crash That Never Happened

It was late June 1947, in the years before satellites and trips to the moon, before space stations and stem cell research. On that early-summer day, nature was ripping through New Mexico with its usual enthusiasm. The air sizzled with ozone, the aftermath of the lightning bolts that tore the sky apart. Thunder had its say as it rumbled through the mountains and crept over the plains. The ranchers had seen and heard it all before, but on this summer day something was different; added to the clanging cacophony of nature was a new sound, one that boomed over the thunder of the storm.

It takes a lot to surprise a rancher. When you live with nature on its lowest level, you learn to accept the unexpected. So although the ranchers noted the sound, none went out into the monsoon storm to locate the cause of it. They figured that they could find out later, when they checked their cattle and their fence lines, whether the big boom had affected them.

It wasn't until days later, in the beginning of July, that Mark Brazel headed out to do just that, to check his pastures, his livestock, and his fence lines. Brazel was the foreman of the Foster Ranch. The ranch raised some cattle but mostly sheep, and it was Brazel's responsibility to oversee this spread. That day he was accompanied by his favorite riding partner, seven-year-old Timmy "Dee" Proctor. It was Dee's dream to be a big-time rancher like Brazel, and he was an enthusiastic partner who often accompanied the cowboy on his rounds. On that fateful day, both Brazel and Dee were to learn much more than they ever dreamed, and it would change their lives forever.

It was July Fourth when Dee and Brazel rode into one of the pastures. Amazingly, it was covered with hundreds of pieces of shiny metal. It looked like pieces of aluminum in sizes ranging from a few inches to a foot or two. When they dismounted and picked up a piece, they were surprised at its lightness. Crumpling the material in their hands was easy because of its thinness and flexibility. However, when they opened their fists, the material sprang back into its original shape. This characteristic of the material astounded both the adult and the child. Because of this amazing peculiarity, the material was given the nickname "memory metal."

In ranch country news travels fast, and some neighbors were able to visit the site. They picked up pieces of the material and carted them home for souvenirs. However, when neighbor

Bud Palmer went to round up a stray near where Brazel had found the debris, military personnel stopped him and escorted him away from the area. In the ensuing days the military clamped down hard on news of what was later described as a UFO crash. Reportedly, in house-to-house searches, the military confiscated the souvenirs and warned people to say nothing of what they saw or knew.

Initially Brazel did not try to keep anything secret. He showed several pieces of the material to friends, who suggested that he report his findings to Frank Wilcox, the Roswell sheriff. Sometime before he made that long ride into Roswell, he visited an adjacent site and found, hidden among more scraps of material, a foreboding secret: bodies. There were at least two, perhaps three of the strangest-looking creatures Brazel had ever seen. Brazel would later refer to them as "little people."

Brazel must have shared the location of the second site with his buddy Dee. In 1994 Dee, now a man, took his family to the site and announced, "This is where Mark found something else," never clarifying what that "something else" was.

Other reports say that this second site, the body site, was already known to military personnel. They had been following unidentified blips on the radar screen for four days. When these blips suddenly disappeared, recorded coordinates led them to this field.

Whatever Brazel knew about these bodies he decided to share with Sheriff Wilcox. Strange thoughts and expectations must have been running through Brazel's mind, for not only did he tell his story to the sheriff, but on the morning of July 6, 1947, he also shared his story with KGFL radio announcer Frank Joyce. He told Joyce about the bodies he had found, saying he was drawn to this site by a strange smell and buzzards circling overhead. Apparently the bodies had lain there for several days, because they had been mutilated by wild animals.

At Wilcox's insistence, he and Brazel contacted personnel at Roswell Army Air Field (RAAF). The army immediately sent personnel out to secure the area and collect the debris. For his report Brazel wound up being the guest of the military for about a week.

Meanwhile, about forty miles north/northwest of Roswell, archaeology students from Texas Tech University were conducting an initial survey for prehistoric sites. On the morning of July 7, 1947, they found something not from the past, but perhaps from the future. Professor William "Curry" Holden hunted down the nearest telephone, which was in Mesa, and called his find into the fire department. He and his students had discovered a strange-looking object, an oblong, disk-shaped pod containing three dead bodies, as well as one that looked alive.

Again military personnel in Roswell were informed of the find. Under the direction of Colonel William Blanchard, the commander of the 509th Bomb Group, Lieutenant Walter G. Haut, the public information officer, issued this press release on July 8:

The many rumors regarding the flying disc became a reality yesterday when the intelligence office of the 509th Bomb Group of the Eighth Air Force, Roswell Army Air Field, was fortunate enough to gain possession of a disc through the cooperation of one of the local ranchers and the sheriff's office of Chaves County. The flying object landed on a ranch near Roswell sometime last week. Not having phone facilities, the rancher stored the disc until such time as he was able to contact the sheriff's office, who in turn notified Maj. Jesse A. Marcel of the 509th Bomb Group Intelligence Office. Action was immediately taken and the disc was picked up at the rancher's home. It was inspected at the Roswell Army Air Field and subsequently loaned by Major Marcel to higher headquarters.

There are a few strange things about this publicity release. First of all, none of the subsequent investigators have found any evidence that Brazel found a pod on his land, or that he stored the disk, although he did store some large pieces of debris. The disk referred to in the press release and attributed to Brazel was probably the pod found by the archaeologists. Second, this release was soon rescinded, and a new release was issued, stating that the object was a crashed weather balloon.

Military activity increased around the three sites—the Brazel debris site, the Brazel body field, and the archaeologists' area. Military men from the base were ordered to clean up the debris and to guard the area. During the cleanup of the sites, the bodies were transported to the base at night or early morning under the most stringent security. Even the men cleaning up the areas had no knowledge of the removal of the bodies, or even that bodies had been found on the sites.

The morning of July 8, Glenn Dennis, a young mortician working at the Ballard Funeral Home, received a strange call from the base inquiring about children's coffins. Unfortunately, the Ballard Funeral Home did not have enough coffins to meet the army's request. In a follow-up call, the army caller asked Dennis for information on how to prepare bodies that had been lying out in the desert for several days and also wanted to know what possible effect the procedures would have on the bodies' systems. Dennis offered to go out to the base and assist them, but the army refused his offer, saying the information was needed only for future use.

Later that day Dennis had business on the base. He had to deliver an injured enlisted man who had been hurt in a motorcycle accident to the base hospital. Ballard Funeral Home had the ambulance contract to transport military personnel who had been injured off base back to the base. He discharged his patient and then drove around to the back of the base infirmary, parking next to another ambulance that was guarded by two MPs. Dennis saw a long, bluish-silver metal object protruding from the back of the open ambulance door.

He went into the hospital to say hello to some of the hospital personnel. Because of his job, he knew many of them well. Having some free time, he was on his way to the lounge for a Coke when he spotted a nurse he knew coming out of one of the examining rooms. She held a cloth over her mouth. When she saw Dennis, she told him, "Get out of here or you're going to be in a lot of trouble." The next day the nurse called the funeral home and told Dennis she needed to talk to him in person.

When they met, she told Dennis she had entered a room to get supplies and found two doctors performing a preliminary autopsy. They asked her to take notes during the procedure. She described the scene as gruesome and the odor as horrible. She told Dennis that the bodies were small, with a disproportionately large head, deep-set eyes, and a concave nose. The doctors noted that there was heavy cartilage in the mouth cavity in place of teeth. Their hairless bodies were black, perhaps due to exposure in the desert.

Apparently the bodies were seen by others, including Lieutenant Governor Joseph Montoya, who was visiting the base; several nurses; and other RAAF personnel who were assigned jobs as guards, debris cleanup crews, and military vehicle drivers, as well as one or two who were walking by when the bodies were being transported between the fields and the base.

The description given by these eyewitnesses varied in some details, but all agreed that the figures were about the size of a ten-year-old, ranging in height from three to four feet. All the eyewitnesses also said that the creatures were smooth-skinned, although one did report that a slight fuzz covered the body. There is, however, some disagreement on the color of the skin. Skin color was reported as ranging from white, to yellow-white, to gray. One or two eyewitnesses even hinted at a green tinge to the skin color.

The witnesses agreed on a few other physical characteristics. The heads were described as larger than the body, with large, slanted eyes; a slight ridge for a nose, with prominent nose holes; and a small slit for a mouth. The creatures had ear holes, but no ears. Several people also said that the arms were thin and long, ending with four-fingered hands.

Later Dennis tried to contact the nurse but was told that she had transferred out. Shortly thereafter, nurses he knew on the base told him that she had died in a plane crash. The fact that he first refused to tell investigators her name, and then admittedly later gave them a false name, taints his testimony.

In the following days, unscheduled air traffic increased on the base. Some witnesses say there were as many as eight flights, but most agree there were three or four. Large crates were seen being loaded into at least two of the planes. On July 8 Major Jesse Marcel, Roswell's army intelligence officer, left RAAF on board a B-29 that reportedly carried a special cargo. Days before, Marcel had viewed the debris field with Brazel and picked up some of the debris, which he transported to the base. Marcel's plane flew to Fort Worth Air Field and returned approximately four or five hours later.

Major Jesse Marcel holding foil material from Roswell, New Mexico, on July 8, 1947. He later told his family that this was not the material he found at the site but some that had been substituted for the picture.

COURTESY *FORT WORTH STAR-TELEGRAM* PHOTOGRAPH COLLECTION, SPECIAL COLLECTIONS, THE UNIVERSITY OF TEXAS AT ARLINGTON LIBRARY, ARLINGTON, TEXAS

On July 9 three C-54s, loaded with crates, packages of debris, and reportedly the bodies, departed the air base. Their destinations were Wright Army Air Field in Ohio; Kirtland Army

Air Field, headquarters of intelligence and research commands; headquarters of the command that oversaw Roswell Army Air Field; and Los Alamos. One of the crewmen on a Fort Worth flight reportedly heard that three strange bodies were being delivered to the Texas base. Some eyewitnesses reported that there was a stopover, or other direct flights to Andrews Air Field near Washington, D.C. The collected crash material and bodies were all transported out of Roswell and were never seen or heard about again.

The base personnel involved in the Roswell crash also disappeared. Some were ordered out almost immediately. Others, because of normal military orders, left the base within the year. In time, public interest in UFOs cooled, fewer sightings were reported, and America got on with its cold war and everyday terrestrial living.

That's the story of the Roswell alien crash as pieced together through interviews, analysis, and conjecture. By the time UFO investigators became interested in the "truth" of the Roswell crash, many eyewitnesses were dead or could not be found, leaving many unanswered questions. Also, investigators found that documents were missing, personnel lists were incomplete, and people's memories of the incident were contradictory.

Not all ufologists agree with the Roswell UFO crash story. Some claim that there was no alien crash and therefore no strange "memory metal" or alien bodies. They maintain that it was all based on incorrect memories and half lies. Psychologists even suggested that events occurring at different times and places are sometimes fused into one memory. Some of the military men did see horrendous crashes with terrible injuries and fatalities during their careers. They could have conceivably combined all these memories into "a Roswell experience."

Other ufologists take apart the Roswell alien crash story point by point using imagination, conjecture, and analyses that sometimes make quantum leaps to connect the dots.

However, there do seem to be a few areas of agreement. Something crashed in Brazel's pasture in either late June or early July. Was it a meteor, an experimental top-secret balloon, or an alien spaceship? Another point of agreement: Brazel did report the crash to Sheriff Wilcox and the military. Lieutenant Walter Haut, the public information officer, did issue a press release about a crashed alien ship that was withdrawn within hours. Major Jesse Marcel did go out to view the crash site and reported back to his superiors with his findings and some samples. And Major Marcel, within days, flew to Wright Air Field in Ohio with material from the crash site. However, the mystery remains, and because it is a mystery, it has few if any answers.

In the 1960s, Hollywood, television, and several UFO investigators revisited the Roswell mystery. The public became so captured by this topic, and so outraged with the thought that the government had covered up the true story, that the government authorized a study of the incident and UFO sightings in general.

The study by the U.S. Air Force, which is called Project Blue Book, looked into UFO sightings and other outer-space phenomena. The air force closed out its investigation in 1969. Among its conclusions were that no UFO that was ever reported presented a threat to the United States and that there have never been any extraterrestrial visitors or equipment on Wright-Patterson Air Force Base (formerly Wright Army Air Field). The government, satisfied with the results of the investigation, declared that the topic of UFOs and extraterrestrial beings was closed for good.

Dissatisfied with the absence of investigation into alien bodies in the Blue Book report, Congressman Steve Schiff of New Mexico asked the U.S. General Accounting Office to look into the matter. The results of this investigation were published in 1997 in *The Roswell Report: Case Closed.* The conclusion was that a significant number of eyewitnesses either misremembered or were creative in their stories; therefore, a conclusion could not be made as to the validity of the claim that alien bodies were found in New Mexico. The report noted the scientific explanation that people will often interweave several events, with the mind adjusting the inconsistencies to form one story. What was reported, said many official sources, was an aircraft crash that was seen at one point in an eyewitness's life, which that individual then incorporated into some fantasies he or she had read or viewed, to form the story of the UFO crash and the alien bodies.

While the science of psychology will support the theory of memory integration in general, there is no proof that it applies in the Roswell crash case. Some people, including Major Marcel's son, insist that they saw material that was unknown at that time.

The public is still not satisfied; the questions have outlasted the investigation results. What happened to the crash material recovered at the Brazel site and to the oval pod? Were alien bodies found, and if so, where are they? And how much of our current aviation and military high technology can be attributed to what was found on that New Mexico land?

In 1948 and 1949 two interesting progress reports were made to the U.S. Air Force at Wright-Patterson Air Force Base on a "memory metal." These reports were submitted by scientists from the Battelle Memorial Institute of Columbus, Ohio, a research institute that did secret work for the government during the 1940s and 1950s. These progress reports concerned the testing and development of a "memory metal." While these citations can still be found in early scientific papers and journals, the actual reports seem to be missing. They cannot be located at the Battelle Institute, Wright-Patterson Air Force Base, or any government depositories, such as the National Archives.

Today we do have a "memory metal," called Nitinol. It is an amalgam of nickel and pure titanium and has shape-recovery characteristics. Titanium is found in outer space. Not only does Nitinol recover its original shape when crumpled, but it is strong, lightweight, silver in color, and will withstand high heat, such as from a blowtorch. Nitinol was officially introduced to the scientific community in 1960.

CHAPTER NINE

The Madness of the Mayberry Murders

The lake's calm surface was teased by a slight breeze that occasionally gathered enough force to gently ripple the surface. Along its shore two fishermen contentedly dozed in the afternoon sun while their lines trailed in the smooth waters.

It was a scene of contentment, a perfect picture of peace and enjoyment. But seventy-five feet beneath the waters of Bonito Lake, buried deep, was the memory of a town. And within that memory seethed the horror of unpremeditated, unexplained, and unpredictable murder.

It all happened more than a century ago when there was no lake. In its place existed a typical mining town. On the frontier in 1885, anyplace with a few tents, a building or two, and the promise of gold was considered a town, but this place was given the grand title of a city. Although Bonito City bore an elite name, it was no more than a village or, if one wanted to be generous, a small town. It had three general stores, a schoolhouse, a post office, a boardinghouse, one blacksmith, one lawyer, and, most importantly, a saloon. The residents were mostly prospectors and the people who served them. Scattered around the countryside were a few farms. Bonito City was in an isolated area, a place of rolling hills covered with tall trees, through which the Rio Bonito wandered.

May 4, 1885, burst forth as a bright and sunny day. Nothing was different or special about this day in Bonito City, nothing to indicate that in the early hours of the next morning the town would face a horror that would be the death of the town.

The town's main road was a winding ribbon of dirt road that worked its way through the hills and trees of Bonito City. On this day the road stirred as a sudden gust of wind kicked up a dust devil. Crossing the road, Dr. William H. Flynn held on to his hat as he headed for the Mayberry Hotel, as the place was called. Truthfully it was really more a boardinghouse than a hotel. It was a family residence with a few rooms to let.

The boardinghouse/hotel was run by Mr. and Mrs. Mayberry. They rented their upstairs bedroom out to accommodate those passing through town, or those who wanted to stay, perhaps trying their hand at prospecting for gold.

Some placer gold was located in the shallows of the Rio Bonito. When word initially got out, the town was inundated by prospectors, professional miners, amateurs, and dreamers. Some didn't stick around very long. Time and hard work took their dreams away. The town quickly became a popular spot for get-rich-quick seekers. So far, no one had hit it big, but the area did have some gold, as flakes and an occasional nugget were brought in.

The Mayberrys had room for two boarders, and Dr. Flynn was one of the guests staying with them. He wasn't there for the gold, nor was he passing through on his way to somewhere else. He was in Bonito City as a favor to a friend.

Flynn was not a local man, or even a westerner. He owned a large drugstore in Boston, but because of ill health he had turned its operation over to his brother and spent the winter of 1884–1885 in Santa Fe. There he stayed at the boardinghouse of Mrs. E. N. Cone. That summer Mrs. Cone thought of setting up a summer place on the Rio Bonito for those wanting to escape the desert heat, and Flynn, along with Mrs. Cone's friends Mr. and Mrs. Burt, journeyed to Bonito City to investigate the possibility of establishing a seasonal hotel there.

Shortly after they arrived in the area, urgent business demanded the return of Mrs. Cone and the Burts to Santa Fe, but Flynn agreed to stay on and look after Mrs. Cone's household effects until her return to Bonito City. Not being prepared for this event, he was pleased when he found a room that seemed to answer all of his needs at the Mayberrys' boardinghouse.

In this busy small town, with prospectors, shopkeepers, and farmers bustling around, Flynn considered himself fortunate when he found such convenient accommodations with amicable people like the well-respected Mayberrys. In a small town where everyone knew everyone else well, their reputation was a good sign that meant a lot to him. After all, this was a mining town and a crossroads for all sorts of dubious and dishonest types of people drifting around the Old West. Most of the drifters were trying to make their fortune in the easiest way possible. A prosperous man had to be careful.

Dr. Flynn's mind was not on gold as he walked up the dusty road on that May day. His thoughts were more on how to protect the things Mrs. Cone had left in his care. He was mulling over several plans. Unfortunately, none of them included protecting himself. He had no need for plans like that. He hardly knew anyone in town, and those he did know seemed pleasantly accepting of him.

The Mayberrys were a family of five: Mr. and Mrs. Mayberry; their son John Jr., who was eighteen years old; his younger brother Edward, age thirteen; and Nellie, their fourteen-year-old daughter.

Dr. Flynn shared his upstairs room with Martin Nelson, who was considered by the townspeople a "good citizen." Nelson was a Swede from Nebraska. He had arrived in Bonito City several years before, just about the time news of a gold strike had spread to the outside world. Nelson said he came to prospect. A few townsfolk noticed that he was not working very hard at it; however, from time to time he had a windfall of money.

It was a strange pairing—the educated doctor and the common laborer—but they seemed to get along well enough. That is, until the early hours of May 5, when Dr. Flynn was awakened by an unusual sound in his room. It was three o'clock in the morning, and the noise woke Dr. Flynn up from a sound sleep. Sitting up in bed, he spotted Nelson going through his pockets. He roared out of bed and advanced on the thief. Nelson spun around; using his pistol, he delivered a blow to the doctor's head. Flynn staggered, giving Nelson time to take aim and shoot the doctor through the heart. Dr. Flynn was dead before he hit the floor.

The gunshots woke the Mayberry family, and all five rushed up the stairs to investigate. John Mayberry and his two sons were the first to arrive on the scene. Calmly, Nelson took aim and shot Mayberry and his sons as they appeared in the doorway of his room. All three died instantly.

Mrs. Mayberry, who was several months pregnant, was not far behind the rest of her family. Calmly, and without remorse or much thought, Nelson shot her twice. Wounded, but still conscious and staggering on her feet, she slipped down the stairs, dragging her daughter Nellie with her in an attempt to get outside to safety. She managed to get out the door but collapsed, mortally wounded, in front of her house, where Nelson caught up with her.

Seeing that Mrs. Mayberry was still alive, Nelson shot her again. The ball not only hit Mrs. Mayberry but also hit Nellie in the side. Nellie managed to struggle to her feet and then ran into the cellar of the adjacent house. Here Nelson cornered her. He drew his gun to finish her off. "Your father, mother, and

brothers are dead. Would you not like to join them in heaven?"
he taunted her. Nellie, shocked and quivering with fear at what
she was facing, pleaded for her life. Finally, Nelson agreed to let
her live if she promised to come to his hanging.

In the town saloon Peter Nelson was cleaning up from
the night's business when he heard the gunshots and shouting.
Although they shared the same last name, and Peter was Swed-
ish, he was no relation to the killer; in fact, Peter barely knew
him. At the first sound of shots, he seized his rifle and took off
for the Mayberry house. The murderer, spotting him, yelled,
"You want one too?" and with that he shot the saloon keeper in
the chest.

The gunshots brought neighbor Hermann Consbruch on
the run. When he spied Mrs. Mayberry's body crumpled by the
front door, he hurried over to her, hoping to give her aid. Gently he lifted her into his arms. Opening her eyes, she whispered,
"Oh, he killed us all." "Who?" asked Consbruch. "Nelson" was
the reply, and with that Mrs. Mayberry died.

The early-morning commotion woke up the village, and
now most of them stood outside the front of the house, thinking
they were trapping the killer inside with the bodies of his victims.
They posted guards, but it was too late. Nelson had already
slipped away to find his horse and more ammunition.

A short distance away he showed up at the Rademachers'
house. Mr. Rademacher was in the village with the other men
looking for Nelson. The killer threatened Mrs. Rademacher

with his gun but told her he would not harm her if she gave him breakfast. The terrified wife complied, and after eating, he told her he had killed the whole Mayberry family and was going back to get more.

While Nelson was crossing the hill that separated the Rademacher house from the village, he spotted Herman Beck, the local grocer, who was standing guard by the house. Thinking that Nelson was still in the house, Beck was facing the log home with his back to Nelson. Now about 250 yards from Beck, Nelson carefully took aim and shot him in the back. It was a killing shot. Nelson's corpses were mounting up.

Nelson took off down the street. As he passed the front of the hotel, he saw Consbruch kneeling by Mrs. Mayberry; Nelson took a quick shot at Consbruch but missed in his haste. He ran around the house firing his rifle randomly at the guards and onlookers. At the guards he kept shouting commands of bravado—"Go to the brush!" and "Hunt your holes!"

Charlie Berry, the justice of the peace, was one of the townsmen who had come to help protect the town. At this point all agreed that Nelson was a killer and a madman and therefore the utmost precaution had to be taken. When Berry spotted Nelson running near the Mayberry home, Berry took careful aim. Meanwhile, Nelson saw Berry raise his rifle. Nelson stopped so that he could get a good shot, raised his rifle, and got the justice of the peace in his sights. But before Nelson could squeeze the trigger and get his shot off, three of the guards let loose a volley.

Nelson, knocked down by the bullets, tried to get to his feet when a fourth bullet hit him. All of the shots were true; any one of them would have killed him. Four of them made a certainty of Nelson's death.

The shocked and mourning town drew itself together and attended to the burials. The townspeople fashioned beautiful trimmed coffins in a good wood. They gave the Mayberrys, Peter Nelson, and Herman Beck honorable burials, placing their graves on a hillside underneath the tall pines near the Mayberry home.

Dr. Flynn's body had a different fate. Dr. Flynn's father arranged for an undertaker to come down from Santa Fe to embalm the body and ready it for shipment back to his home in Boston. The doctor's body was kept on ice until the mortician arrived. When the body was embalmed, it was sent by stagecoach to the town of Carthage, fourteen miles away, where it was to be placed on a train for Boston. Unfortunately, torrential rains in the area caused the stagecoach to miss the train by six minutes. The railroad employees then placed Dr. Flynn's body on a hand-car and pumped eight miles on the tracks in the blinding rain to reach the town of San Antonio so that Dr. Flynn's body could catch the train to Boston.

Martin Nelson's body was not given the care or the reverent treatment of his victims. It was carelessly thrown facedown into a rough pine box and buried with his feet pointing west. (It was the belief of the day that bodies needed to be buried face up and pointing toward the east so that they could rise and join Christ at the Second Coming.)

Mrs. Rademacher took care of the wounded Nellie Mayberry, nursing her back to health until she was well enough to travel. Then, accompanied by her uncle, Nellie left for her relatives' home in Iowa. The town of Bonito City never heard from Nellie Mayberry again.

As the town slowly recovered from the horror of the Mayberry massacre, the people of Bonito City tried to find an explanation for this senseless event. Some of the townspeople remembered that Nelson was not an industrious worker. They also recalled that a series of petty robberies had taken place in the area, after which Nelson always had money.

The women of the town, speculating on romance, said that Nelson was enamored with Nellie but that Mr. Mayberry frowned on the romance. "He was stealing the watch," some said, "so he could run away with Nellie." And so the guesses continued, with no one able to come up with a true answer.

If Nelson was out to just steal the watch or whatever was in Dr. Flynn's pockets, why did he not just knock the doctor unconscious and in the quiet of the night make his getaway? Why did he kill the Mayberrys? There was talk that Nelson wanted no witnesses to his crime. But the additional gunshots woke the whole town, and even in his shooting rampage he could not kill everyone.

It is also strange that after escaping the house where the crimes were committed, he returned. His remark to Mrs.

Rademacher—that he wanted to go back to "get two or three more"—sounded like the ravings of a madman.

Before the killings, the townspeople had looked on Nelson as an upstanding citizen. What changed him? Was it love, the unrequited love of Nellie? Was it hatred for people who had something when he had so little? Or was it as simple as madness?

The brutal murders of seven people on that morning of May 5 represented more than the slaughter of innocent people; it sounded the death knell for Bonito City. Families began leaving town. Some believed they were no longer safe in this isolated place. Others needed to get away from the memory of that horrible night that took their friends.

Not all moved on. Hermann Consbruch, the man who tried to save Mrs. Mayberry, stayed in Bonito City. On April 18, 1901, he was appointed the postmaster, a position he held for eight years. He served the town longer than any other postmaster.

Five years later the gold ore was all but gone, and by 1910 the census showed that only two people lived in Bonito City. In 1911 the post office, which also served the outlying area of farms and scattered villages, closed, and in 1920 the once busy town consisted of only a store and a few houses.

By 1920 the Southern Pacific Railroad was running steam engine trains throughout the Southwest. The number of trains had increased to the extent that the supply of water was no longer sufficient. The railroad turned its eyes to Rio Bonito. Southern Pacific received permission from the government to dam the creek to form a reservoir. The railroad then negotiated with the few people who still lived in the area for the land around the lake. The remaining residents were more than glad to sell and move on. The water from Bonito Lake, as the reservoir was now called, would answer the steam engines' thirsty demands, and the isolated Bonito City was a perfect spot for replenishing the engines' water supplies.

Slowly over the years, the water in Bonito Lake rose. In 1933 the Pfingsten family, who had lived in the area for many years, noticed that the water level was approaching the graves of Nelson and the people he murdered, which were located on the little hillside of the lake. The Pfingstens took it upon themselves to dig up the bodies for reinterment. At this time any remaining evidence of the town was also removed.

Nelson's victims were given new caskets and with great reverence buried in a common grave on a hill in the nearby town of Angus, New Mexico, which is not too far from Bonito Lake. Nelson was not treated so tenderly. When the Pfingstens dug up his bones, they noted that his green felt hat was intact. They jammed his bones and the hat back into a coffin and again dumped his body, this time about fifty feet above the road at the base of the hill where his victims were buried. They marked his grave with a concrete tombstone.

Today, though the plot is overgrown from lack of care and hard to find, Nelson's tombstone serves as a historical marker of a mysterious murder rampage, one that still puzzles researchers.

The grave stone of the Mayberry family. R. F. Oswald was not a victim but the small son of the Oswalds who died and was reburied with the Mayberrys when the graves were removed from Bonito Lake.

Beneath the beautiful calm waters of Bonito Lake, all evidence of the former town has been removed. The only thing that could not be taken away was the memory of what happened in the early-morning hours of May 5, 1885, to seven innocent people.

When the waters of Bonito Lake were no longer needed for steam engines, the lake took on a new purpose. It became the drinking-water source for nearby communities. It is still a beautiful spot, and while fishing is permitted, boating, swimming, and wading are not. If you do break the law and seek the cool waters of Bonito Lake for a quick swim, be careful. You just might feel a ghostly hand brushing your foot.

CHAPTER TEN

The Half Man

It was a clear spring day on May 12, 2009, when two old friends decided to take a ride. The New Mexican man wanted to show the countryside off to his out-of-state friend. They drove down to Window Rock, Arizona, and then headed back to Farmington, New Mexico, via the little-used Narbona Pass. It was nearing five o'clock, and both men were looking forward to having dinner. They were zipping along at sixty-five miles an hour, the skies were bright, the sun was shining, and the visibility was so clear that they felt they could see forever. There was no other traffic to take their minds off the views.

As the car rounded a curve, something on the hillside caught the driver's attention. On the east side of the road, just where the forest met the meadow, there was movement; something was working its way diagonally up the side of the hill.

The driver slowed and said, "Did you see that?" When the other man replied that he had, the driver hit the brakes, intending to back up and get another look. But by this time, whatever they had seen was gone. They compared notes. Not having to concentrate on driving, the passenger had the best view of the strange sight. However, both agreed that whatever they saw was walking on two legs and was larger than any black bear or elk they had ever spotted. The creature was covered with long, blackish-brown hair that hung down from a body that was at least seven feet tall.

What they saw was about fifty yards from the road, and the observation had lasted for only five or so seconds. The creature moved along with large strides and used its right arm to grab trees to help pull itself up the hill. It appeared to be carrying something in its left arm, but the witnesses did not get a good view of the object. Whatever it was that they saw, both men were convinced it was no animal they were familiar with.

It was a strange encounter, but not an isolated incident, for this was in the Chuska mountain range of northwestern New Mexico, and many unusual sightings had been reported there over the years.

One of the first sightings in the Chuskas of this strange creature was reported in the summer of 1980. A Navajo family saw a grayish-brown creature kneeling near their well. They knew it wasn't a bear, for they had never seen a bear kneeling, and this figure seemed to be either washing something or drinking from the well.

In 1998 several locals noticed something large, described as "a brownish red hairy thing that stinks to high heaven and makes some god-awful noises," stalking along the San Juan River. Again in the spring of 2002, a strange being was spotted in the wilderness area of the San Juan River. It was described as being a bipedal with long, dark hair covering its tall body.

Then in June of that year, a young man riding in the back of a truck with his family got a good look at a creature that he described as being "as tall as the cedar trees . . . with hair covering its whole body with a mixture of grey/dark brown and white on its chest. The head and feet, also the hands, were all dark in color and the legs were dark grey. The face was lighter in color and when I saw the face it was turned toward my direction. The forehead was most unusual and it really stuck out with no neck. It had a little slump in the shoulder and its arms spanned down to its knees. It took large steps and its arms swung back and forth."

In 2005 two more creature incidents were reported in the Chuska Mountains, including one from a zoologist who heard unusual knocking noises that were definitely not made by a woodpecker.

That summer an even more bizarre event occurred. About 2:00 a.m. a family camping in the Chuska Mountains felt something bumping into the nylon ropes used to secure the tent's rain cover. The rope was pulled and snapped back several times. Muffled footsteps were heard and then some scraping noises on the rain cover as if someone was running fingernails over the material. The rain cover began flapping as though its ground stakes had been pulled up. Suddenly more footsteps were heard, these off to the southeast of the tent about ten feet away.

The clatter of rocks coming from the northeast indicated that something was moving away. All this action took place in a twenty-minute time frame. When things quieted down, the campers went out to take a look. Two rain cover stakes had been pulled up. A further investigation turned up an eight-inch-long footprint.

All these sightings were in or near the Chuska mountain range, which lies within the Navajo Reservation, north of Gallup, New Mexico. The elevation here is between 8,000 and 9,000 feet. Inhabiting this isolated area are various types of wildlife: mule deer, elk, black bear, mountain lions, bobcats, and coyotes. The region is heavily forested with ponderosa pine, aspen, gamble oak, spruce, and fir, and many small seasonal lakes dot the land.

The Chuska mountain range is not the only area in New Mexico that has had visits from this strange creature. Since 1976 there have been at least thirty-two reported sightings in various locations in New Mexico. The number of encounters that have gone unreported can't be estimated. Some who did report incidents mentioned that they knew others who had seen or heard these strange beasts but had never reported them.

Isolated sightings have been reported in Lincoln, Colfax, McKinley, Sandoval, Taos, and Dona Ana counties. All these encounters occurred during various months and times of the year, and all but one were in wooded mountainous areas.

The non-mountain sighting took place near Las Cruces in the fall of 2001. A teenager camping with his family over Thanksgiving week caught a glimpse of an eight-foot-tall creature walking in the moonlight through the ravine. Terrified, he ran into the trailer and told his family, who thought it was quite a laughing matter. To appease the boy, however, an older brother was sent outside with a flashlight to inspect the area.

At first the two boys saw nothing. Then they heard an angry growl and shuffling in the dirt such as a bull makes just before it charges. The frightened boys ran into the trailer, falling through the doorway in their haste. They were scared out of their minds. While Las Cruces is not in the mountains, the mountains are less than an hour away.

The most reported sightings of this strange beast come from Otaro County. The Sacramento Mountains are in this county, which covers an area of 720 square miles, with elevations from 5,400 to 12,000 feet. Since 1976 ten sightings in Otaro have been recorded. The latest Otaro encounter occurred near the town of Mescalero in March 2008.

It was a restless night for the woman. As she couldn't sleep, she decided to watch TV. While she sat there, the feeling that something was watching her caused her to look toward the window. Turning her head, she saw a dark figure peering at her through the window. Its huge shape was backlit by an outside motion-sensing floodlight placed about eighteen feet up on the wall. Hoping to scare the figure away, she turned the volume up on the TV, and after five or six minutes the shadow moved away.

The frightened woman phoned her brother to come out and take a look; because the creature seemed to have left, he told her that he would wait until the morning to come. The next day they inspected the ground around the house and saw the tracks in the snow—footprints that measured between fourteen and sixteen inches in length.

This family had lived in this area for more than ten years. During that time there had been many unexplained incidents, including the killing of several dogs. Also they reported that they had frequently heard vocalizations consisting of loud, unidentified screams.

One of the most frightening experiences happened to a camper in 1983 near Cuba, New Mexico, about seven miles into the Santa Fe National Forest. The young man was on a camping trip with fellow students from the Southwest Indian Polytechnic Institute in Albuquerque. He was alone in his tent when about 4:00 a.m. he was awakened by a terrible stench that actually burned his nostrils. He sat up in his sleeping bag and saw a massive light-brown hairy arm reach through the front flap into his tent. The arm probed the inside of the tent as if it was searching for something. The arm was covered in a furry pelt that stopped at the wrist, with only dark skin covering the hand. The nails were about four inches long and were the color of candle wax. The young man described the hand as measuring about fourteen inches from wrist to fingertips and about nine inches in width. The camper was so terrified that he began to hyperventilate and was about to scream when the arm abruptly withdrew.

Cautiously peering outside the tent, the camper saw two figures revealed by the dim light. One was significantly larger than the other. Their vocalizations, consisting of grunts, groans, gurgling sounds, and subdued screams, were delivered in two different pitches, leading the camper to believe that one figure was male and the other female. Making what sounded like Indian hooting sounds, the creatures hurriedly left the campsite.

These encounters and others were investigated by an organization of cryptozoologists (those who search for elusive animals) that was formed in January 1982. It is directed by a board of zoologists from various subdisciplines. Out of this organization came the Bigfoot Field Researchers Organization (BFRO), which records and investigates reported encounters with unusual vocalizations, spoor, or footprints, as well as visuals of unidentified creatures.

The BFRO has investigated sightings all over the United States, with most occurring in the North and Southwest. In New Mexico the vast majority of these sightings were made on or near Indian reservations by Native Americans. Could these sightings be an example of mass hysteria? The Native American culture historically includes mythological or religious figures of a huge, hairy, wild woodsman. Circumstances such as stress, fear, or weather conditions could color an encounter with a known animal, turning it into a strange experience. Could the creatures that were seen be nothing more than black bears? These animals are capable of walking on two feet for short distances.

The bear theory, however, does not explain the many strange footprints discovered in New Mexico, Washington, and California and throughout the rest of the world. Some of these places are not inhabited by black bears. Also, most of these sightings have been reported by experienced outdoorsmen who are familiar with bear, elk, and other wild animals.

As for the huge prints, footprints in mud, snow, or soft earth can be weathered by wind, sun, and rain, expanding them and changing the prints to create a large and unknown spoor. Is that what is happening? Are what is being seen really the prints of bear, elk, or another known animal that have been changed beyond recognition? Scientifically

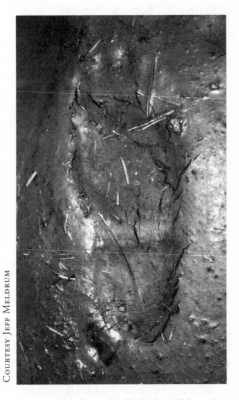

COURTESY JEFF MELDRUM

A 14-inch footprint displaying midtarsal pressure ridges, discovered in the foothills of the Blue Mountains of southeastern Washington by Paul Freeman and examined by Dr. Jeff Meldrum in February 1996.

analyzed casts of these strange footprints, some with very clear foot ridges, have led to the conclusion that most cannot be classified as known animal prints.

Is this creature then a species of a hitherto unclassified North American ape? Sightings, however, have been made in other countries, including Nepal, Russia, Indonesia, and Canada. What then are people seeing?

This mysterious being is called by many names: Yeti, Sasquatch, the Abominable Snowman, and Bigfoot. It has been sighted around the world but has never been found. In New Mexico its yowls vibrate in the canyons, its shadow has been spotted swaggering among the trees, and stories of this creature have been around for decades. But is this creature real, a figment of the imagination, or a fake?

Unfortunately there are always fakers who try to perpetuate a mystery and gain some fame and perhaps fortune in the process. The Bigfoot phenomenon is no exception. Throughout the years, body casts, footprint casts, and a few voice recordings have been produced along with wild tales.

The zoology world was rocked when Caterpillar operator Jerry Crew showed up in 1952 at the local taxidermist with a cardboard outline of a large footprint. Crew was an operator for the Wallace Brothers contractors and worked on a mountain site in Bluff Creek, California. He had discovered the footprints near his machinery on the construction site. They were like none the taxidermist and tracker, Bob Titmus, had ever seen. Crew was given materials to create a plaster cast of the footprints, which were still visible at the site. Crew also reported that fifty-gallon drums of diesel fuel had been moved from the site up the mountain to an off-road, a feat that would require unusual strength.

The casts were analyzed by wildlife experts, who admitted that the prints matched no known animal; but other than that, they reached no conclusions. Later, Ray Wallace, owner of the construction company, admitted that the whole episode was a hoax he had perpetrated to keep casual visitors away from the building site. Wallace had paid $50 for a pair of carved feet that he used to make the prints.

Vocalizations can also be faked. Several recordings of supposed Bigfoot sounds have been analyzed. While some sounds matched the vocalization of known animals, several could not be identified. One of the first things that sound experts look for is manipulation of the recording. If the sound proves true, they then try to compare the recording with known animal sounds, most especially apes, chimpanzees, and other primates. In a few cases, there was no match, and these sounds remain a mystery.

Among all the hoaxes and mysteries, one piece of evidence has defied all expert analysis and to this date seems the most compelling evidence that a Bigfoot creature does exist. It is the Patterson-Gimlin film.

Rancher and builder Bob Gimlin and his fellow rodeo rider Roger Patterson were so captivated by the legends of Bigfoot that they decided to mount an expedition in the northern mountains of California to search for Bigfoot. Armed with enough camping supplies for two weeks, including a 16-mm Kodak camera, they set out with two saddle horses and a pack horse. They set up a base camp at Bluff Creek.

About midday on October 20, 1967, they started out on a search for signs of the elusive creature. They rode upstream along Bluff Creek and skirted a large fallen tree. As they rounded the obstruction, they came to a logjam caused by a previous flood. And there, standing on the creek's bank only sixty to eighty feet away, was a creature the likes of which they had never seen.

Later Gimlin recounted that when he first saw it, "it was standing, looking straight at us. That's when everything started happening. The horses started jumping around, raising the devil and spooking."

Patterson, whose horse was spinning around, was still able to reach into his saddlebag and snare his camera. He fell off his horse and ran across the creek to a sandbar, filming as he went. Meanwhile, the creature turned away and started retreating up the sandbar parallel to the creek bed. The result of this encounter was a film that is still being critiqued and analyzed by experts in various scientific and professional fields. It has been studied by anthropologists, zoologists, and film experts.

There have been attempts to re-create the film using a human in an ape suit, but it was concluded that the clear view of the body muscles of the mysterious creature precluded a man in a costume. Janos Prohaska, noted Hollywood costume designer, believed that in place of a suit, the hair could have been glued directly to the actor's skin, a process that would have taken more than ten hours to complete and is untested.

Accidentally, the film speed was set at 18 frames per second, which produced fuzzier pictures but eliminated the possibility of fakery because it captured a pattern of walking motion that a human being could not possibly duplicate. Dr. Don Grieve, professor of biomechanics at London's Royal Free Hospital of Medicine, who analyzed the film, concluded that the Bigfoot creature possessed a different locomotor system than do humans. Also, Dr. Dmitri Donskoy, of the USSR Central Institute of Physical Culture in Moscow, believes that such a walk, as demonstrated by the film's creature, is absolutely not typical of humans.

Not all the scientists who viewed the film became believers. Some reserved judgment, hoping for some future conclusive evidence, and some were downright doubters.

In 1972 Dr. John Napier, a primatologist, evaluated the Patterson-Gimlin film. He came to this emphatic conclusion: "There is little doubt that the scientific evidence taken collectively points to a hoax of some kind. The creature shown in the film does not stand up well to functional analysis. There are too many inconsistencies; yet no scientist to whom I have spoken and who has seen the film has any direct evidence to prove that the episode was anything other than what it purported to be." Dr. Napier remained a doubter and concluded that while he could not see the zipper (in the costume), he was still not a believer.

Roger Patterson died in 1972. Until the day he died, he maintained that the footage was not a hoax but rather contained the images of a real Bigfoot. Bob Gimlin, who lives in Yakima, Washington, insists that the footage is authentic.

And there the matter remains. With footprint casts that cannot be identified, a film that cannot be disproven, and mounting evidence of sightings and vocalizations, there is still no definitive proof that a Bigfoot creature lives and roams New Mexico's mountains and the world's forests.

Is this half man one of the best-perpetrated hoaxes of our time? Or is it an elusive species still waiting to be discovered?

CHAPTER ELEVEN

A Ghostly Assortment of Dubious Characters

G hosts seem to have a variety of reasons for hanging around. Sometimes they are having too much fun to go on to where they are supposed to be. Not all ghosts, however, are jovial. A few are more unsettled, even violent. And of course some spirits are on a mission. But whatever their reasons for existing, ghosts offer some good scares, a few good laughs, and a lot of mystery.

The Cloudcroft Lodge, 1930

Rebecca tucked a strand of wayward red hair into place, straightened her shirtwaist bodice, and took one last look in the mirror. Satisfied with what she saw, she quietly slipped out of the hotel room, leaving her latest lover sound asleep.

Not expecting to see anyone in the hall at this predawn hour, she was startled when a figure moved from the shadows to stand in front of her.

"What are you doing here?" she demanded, somewhat annoyed at his unexpected appearance.

"Don't you remember, Becky? I live here when I'm not on the logging site."

"Of course I remember. I didn't expect you back so soon."

"That's obvious. Who is the man you just left?"

"Don't be silly," an indignant Rebecca replied. "I was just checking the room."

"Don't lie to me. You couldn't wait until I was gone, could you? How many other men are there? And all this time you kept telling me there was only me and how lonesome you were when I was gone. You're an all-service maid, ain't you?" Suddenly the lumberjack's seemingly placid attitude changed to one of pure anger. Red-faced and breathing hard, he struck Rebecca across the face. His anger knew no bounds, and the brute of a man incessantly hit her until the beautiful redhead was lying lifeless at his feet.

Seeing her still form broke the fog of his fury. Realizing he had murdered the hotel maid, he needed to dispose of the body. Lifting the corpse, he quietly left the hotel and walked into the woods behind the building. He buried the body, covered the grave, and left town. He was never seen again. Rebecca's body has never been recovered, but apparently Rebecca has.

Rebecca was hired as a chambermaid in the 1930s and assigned a room in the basement, where the help had their sleeping quarters. She was a flirtatious woman who loved fun—and loved love. As a beautiful woman, she had plenty of takers to supply both at the hotel. She is still having fun.

Her favorite targets are the new employees at the Cloud-croft Lodge. One such employee, Nosi Crosby, was tending bar on the ground floor one day and needed to use the bathroom. She decided to use the one in the basement. Both stalls were empty. She picked one, and once in the stall, she realized there was no paper on the roll. "Damn," she muttered, "there's no toilet paper." An almost transparent white hand reached under the partition from the next stall, holding a roll of paper. Crosby tore out of the stall, the bathroom, and the basement. For the longest time she refused to go down there. Now when the employees have to go downstairs, they loudly call out to Rebecca, letting her know they are on their way.

Rebecca doesn't confine her tricks to just the basement. The hallways, certain rooms, and the Red Dog Saloon are also her favorites. When alive, she plied her trade in room 101, which is now the Governor's Suite, and that is one of her favorite haunts. Chronic problems plague the phone system there. Calls come from the room when no one is staying in it. Guests in that room sometimes find that their shoes go missing, only to turn up in another guest's room.

The Red Dog Saloon was another of Rebecca's favorite places when she worked at the hotel. Rebecca loved to dance, and on several occasions the cleaning crew has seen a lively redhead twirling around the Red Dog's dance floor in the dimly lit bar area. Here ashtrays move of their own accord, and the fireplace bursts into flame without any obvious fuel. Throughout the hotel, doors open and shut, lights go on and off, and appliances start up on their own.

One male guest returned to his room and found a beautiful and very naked redhead taking a bath in his tub. Rather embarrassed, he called the desk and reported that some woman had mistaken his room for hers and requested that someone come and remove her. When help came, she was gone.

It's no wonder that Rebecca has chosen not to leave the inn. Its setting is spectacular. Located on a mountaintop in the Sacramento Mountains, the elegant three-story ski lodge is in the style of a European Victorian lodge. The original lodge opened in 1899, catering to the lumberjacks for the Alamogordo and Sacramento Railroad. Over the years it has had a series of owners and undergone periods of renovation. Its guest book reads like a historical who's who and includes such names as Pancho Villa, Judy Garland, Clark Gable, and many past Mexican and U.S. government officials.

The Cloudcroft Lodge is still a popular stop where guests are cosseted in rooms furnished in antiques. Its two-story lobby is filled with comfortable soft leather chairs, tasteful antiques, and crystal chandeliers, all of which provide a beautiful setting for modern-day guests—and a lovely ghost.

Fort Union, 1800

The exhausted rider raced into Fort Union and slid from the back of his horse. "The Apaches are on the attack," he yelled as he scurried to the commanding officer's quarters.

A detachment of cavalry was given orders to mount up and find and punish the marauding Apaches. A rather naive and young lieutenant was put in charge.

Before he left, he sought out the sister-in-law of the captain. She was young and quite taken with the attention the men at the fort showered on her. This lieutenant was only one of many.

The lieutenant found the pretty young woman and told her of his love. She admitted she returned his affection and promised him that if anything happened to him, she would never marry— passionate words spoken in a dramatic moment.

"That is well." He promised, "Nobody else shall have you. I will come back and make my claim." Days later the detachment returned without the lieutenant. He was reported missing and possibly dead.

The young lady mourned briefly but soon found a young man from the East who took her fancy. They decided to marry at the post. The wedding day arrived, and all of Fort Union celebrated this grand occasion. The evening ball took place in the mess hall, which had been festively decorated for the occasion.

The bride and groom were whirling around the floor in their wedding dance when the front door banged opened. There, framed by the moonlight, was the swollen body of a dead man. He wore the stained and tattered uniform of a soldier. His eyes were open, staring sightless, and his temple was sliced by a hatchet gash. Silently he moved toward the bride, taking her out of the arms of her husband.

The musicians, beyond their control, began playing a frantic waltz. The beat grew faster and faster, and the couple kept pace. The bride grew pale as the music continued, and she was whirled around and around until she suddenly dropped to the floor, dead. The soldier looked at her for a moment and then emitted a sorrowful cry as he disappeared through the door. A few days later a troop of soldiers returned from the scene of the Apache attack, bringing with them the body of the young lieutenant. His head bore the mark of an Apache hatchet.

Refined young ladies were a rarity on the frontier, and when one did appear, she was treated like a unique beauty and a princess. Soldiers fawned over her, and this kind of attention soon gave some women an exaggerated opinion of themselves and less sensitivity toward others.

In 1851 Fort Union was typical of the army's outposts in Indian country: isolated, primitive, and lonesome. It was built to guard the Santa Fe Trail in the wilderness of Mora Valley. From 1851 until 1891 the fort protected travelers on the trail and the inhabitants of the meager settlements in the area. The army waged many battles with the Apaches, who claimed a right to the land and fought to keep the invaders out.

In a letter home, after he left camp, a private described the fort and its life: "The fort was located in a dreary, treeless and practically grassless plain. Our life in garrison at Fort Union was monotonous and uninteresting. The fort of adobe quarters for officers and men faced a square which contained a star-shaped earthwork in the center with a few mounted cannon."

A Santa Fe trader saw the fort differently in 1857: "Fort Union, a hundred and ten miles from Santa Fe, is situated in the pleasant valley of the Moro. It is an open post, without stockades or breastworks of any kind, and barring the officers and soldiers who are seen about, it has much more the appearance of a quiet frontier village than that of a military station."

Today the site of Fort Union is listed as a National Monument by the National Park Service. What is left of the broken walls and foundation mounds give a mere sense of what the fort used to be. Yet a visit to the Fort Union National Monument can stir feelings of the loneliness and deprivation of life in the frontier forts. However, whatever you do on your visit, don't dance.

El Capitan Peak, the Guadalupe Mountains, 1869

The mountains and the land belonged to the Mescalero Apaches, and they used the caves, canyons, and peaks as a safe haven after their raids on the adjoining ranches and settlements. As the years passed, the land drew more settlers, and the Mescaleros became bolder and crueler. The loss of cattle from the Indians' raids climbed, and the number of attacks on settlers increased. It was time the pioneers got some help. An appeal went out to the army.

In the winter of 1869, Lieutenant Howard B. Cushing arrived with a troop of sixty-five cavalrymen and civilians. They began their campaign by entering the northern part of the Guadalupe Mountains and tracking the Mescaleros to their campground, where in a fierce battle they killed dozens of Mescaleros and routed the rest. The survivors fled to the plains below the mountains. The dominance of the Apaches had been broken, and the Mescalero Apaches were gone from the Guadalupe Mountains.

Yet, in the ensuing years, the throbbing of the Indians' drums could be heard coming from caves in the mountains. In the evening the flicker of campfires spotted the mountains. When a few brave souls went to investigate, they found no evidence of campfires or Indians. Empty caves greeted them, but as they rode away, the drumbeats followed them.

Even many years before, when the Mescaleros called the mountains their home, strange drumbeats and chanting were heard. The Indians knew they were the ghosts of ancestors and were too superstitious to investigate. And so they remained a mystery until a band of Warm Springs Apaches came for a visit.

The Apaches heard ghostly sounds coming from the base of the mountain. Following the sounds, they traced them to a cave just above the canyon floor. In the group of visitors was a medicine woman. Bravely she entered the cave, telling her companions to wait for her at the mouth of the cave. Her escorts settled in on a low rise near the cave mouth and prayed for this brave, and foolish, woman.

After about an hour the Apaches heard the drumbeats. The drums were accompanied by singing, which started out faintly and then increased in volume until the canyon walls shook. Truly frightened, the Indians were sure the medicine woman had been killed by the Earth People who inhabited the cave.

Still they waited. A long time passed, and the Apaches reluctantly made the decision to return to their camp. The Indian woman was surely dead, killed by the Earth People. As they sadly prepared to leave, they heard the medicine woman call to them from deep inside the cave. They cautiously crept nearer, peering into the black depths of the cave, when the woman emerged. In her arms she carried a pure white lamb.

The Earth People, she said, had instructed her to prepare for an important ceremony. It was a ceremony for young, chaste Apache girls. Only the young girls, their relatives, friends, and holy men and women of the tribe were allowed to attend the celebration. This ceremony was a celebration of the sacredness of producing life, which was a gift to the women of the tribe.

The celebration lasted four days. While the holy men and women prayed and sang for the young women, the others beat the drums. The girls danced in a circle around the holy ones while the other guests circled in the opposite direction. This ceremony, which ensures the future of the tribe, is still practiced today, and because of this ritual gift from the Earth People, the Guadalupe Mountains are sacred to the Mescaleros.

However, the haunting drumbeats and the whispered chants are not reserved for just the Native Americans. If they listen very carefully, people passing near the base of the mountains in the early evening can still hear the pounding of the drums, accompanied by faint chanting. Sometimes they even see the campfires of the Mescaleros' ancestors.

St. James Hotel, 1880

The portly gambler smugly laid his cards out on the table. "Read 'em and weep, boys. That pot is mine," he crowed. T. James Wright greedily reached for the pile in the center of the table. A few gold coins scattered, but he gave them no attention. His eyes were fixed on the paper atop the money. It was the deed to the St. James. Wright had just won himself a hotel.

The gambler stood up, carefully tucking the deed into his shirt pocket; he distributed the money into several other pockets. "That's it for me, gentlemen. I hope you sleep as soundly tonight as I will in my hotel." With that, he arrogantly left the room.

Wright slept a lot sounder than he planned; he was shot in the back just as he opened the door to his room. The force of the shot propelled him into the room, where, facedown, he slowly bled to death.

Not at all happy about his missed chance to own a big-time hotel, Wright is still hanging around in room 18, and he acts out his anger on innocent guests. He has been known to push people down who enter his room, spin his room chandelier, and even manifest himself as an angry, huge ball of orange light.

The wise owners have locked the room, barring it from any curious guests. To keep their permanent guest happy, they have left the furnishings as they were in the late 1800s. An iron bed without a mattress dominates the room. On a small table a poker hand, a shot glass, and a bottle of Jack Daniels share space with a tin of Copenhagen chewing tobacco, as well as a few photographs of bikini-clad lovelies (a thoughtful modern touch by the management).

While Wright might be alone in his room, his spirit is not alone in the St. James. Mary Elizabeth Lambert, wife of Henry Lambert, who started the establishment in 1880, drifts through the hallways, checking to see that everything is in order for her contemporary guests. Her children were born in the hotel, and she lived there until her death in December 1926. She still takes her responsibilities seriously in what was her home.

She especially oversees room 17, the room where she lived and where her children were born. If the guest in that room opens the window to let the evening air in, Mary incessantly taps on the glass until the occupant closes the window completely. No chilling night air for her guests.

Mrs. Lambert is not the only family member to enjoy the accommodations of the St. James. Her two-and-a-half-year-old son Johnnie races down the hallways, sits at the bar and spins bottles, and generally uses the hotel as his playground. He was spotted by a young man cleaning up the bar. Thinking he was a guest, the cleanup man asked him to go back to his room, at which point the lad looked up at him, displaying a face horribly scarred from burns. Little Johnnie had died from severe burns after a pot of fried foods tipped over on him.

Johnnie has plenty of playmates. In the late 1800s two little girls, ages twelve and nine, died of diphtheria. Being extremely polite spirits, they disapprove of Johnnie's raucous behavior.

The St. James is home to a number of ghostly guests. A small old man loves pulling tricks on the owners and guests. One time he stuck a knife between the feet of the two owners. He delights in making things disappear and placing them where they should not be, or relighting candles that have been snuffed out. This little imp's favorite targets are the new employees. He once sat himself down at the bar and laughingly tormented and terrorized the new bartender.

A mysterious cowboy was seen one evening in the dining room mirror, but not in the room. Items fall off the shelves, the electronic equipment at the front desk is unpredictable, and cold spots appear and disappear around the hotel.

It is not surprising that so many otherworldly guests inhabit the hotel. The St. James has always been a popular place, and a home to both honorable and questionable guests. At least twenty-six of them met their death within this adobe structure.

St. James Hotel in Cimarron, New Mexico, a favorite haunt of ghostly guests.

The hotel, originally called the Lambert Inn, was built as a saloon in 1872 by Henry Lambert, personal chef to President Abraham Lincoln. After Lincoln's assassination Henry headed west and opened up the saloon.

The establishment was a success, but so many of Henry's customers passed out from the sheer pleasure of drinking at his bar that he added rooms in 1880. Located in the heart of Cimarron and surrounded by the large Maxwell Land Grant, the hotel prospered. It soon became a favorite stop for such notables as Black Jack Ketchum, an outlaw and a train robber; the gunfighter Clay Allison, who danced naked on the bar; Jesse James; and the Earp brothers. Billy the Kid stopped here, as did his killer, Pat Garrett. Doc Holliday, a gambler and a gunfighter;

artist Frederic Remington; and writers Zane Grey and Governor Lew Wallace (author of *Ben-Hur*) also graced the place. Even Buffalo Bill Cody took a liking to the hotel. It was here that he and Annie Oakley planned the Wild West shows.

In the early days of the St. James, the West was quite lawless. Violence was a way of life, and with so many notables around, it could be a dangerous place. When Henry's sons replaced the roof in 1901, they counted more than four hundred bullet holes in the ceiling. A double floor had been laid on the second floor to protect the sleeping guests from stray bullets from below.

The ghosts of the St. James Hotel are more than the figments of imagination. Psychics have actually identified many of the ghosts, and the hotel is considered one of the most haunted places in America.

Nageezi

Fewer than four hundred people live in this New Mexico town, and that doesn't include the ghosts. Counting the spirits would probably double the population. No one really knows why this spot is so popular with these spectral visitors.

The village is populated mostly by young Native Americans (the median age is twenty-six and a half). This somewhat isolated community is located in San Juan County, about one hundred miles northwest of Albuquerque. It sits at an altitude of almost 7,000 feet.

Maybe it is the isolation that appeals to the ghostly visitors, or maybe it is the blatant acceptance by the local residents. For some harassed ghosts, Nageezi could be the perfect vacation spot, offering no stress and a chance to do whatever they want, like the chained-up gentleman who around midnight sits gazing out at the panoramic view of the Huerfano Mountain. Then there is the ghostly hobo who likes to wander around the Ben Detention Dam.

A haggard old woman does her shopping as she staggers around the aisles of a local store. Locals insist that she is the struggling ghost of a former resident. A sobbing gentleman is often found sitting on a park bench after midnight, his chest marked by a big hole.

For the sheer fright factor, a female with a bear's head is frequently seen in the predawn hours looking out over the Aztec Ruins National Monument. This ghost likes to scare people who are unwise enough to disturb the silence of Nageezi.

If you are looking for someplace different, you might want to join these shades of the past in this tiny town and share their ghostly activities.

CHAPTER TWELVE

The Stairs from Heaven

The silence of the chapel was broken by the faint clicks of beads rubbing against each other. Over the cadence could be heard the soft murmur of the nuns as they chanted their novena to St. Joseph. It was a novena offered through hopelessness. The Sisters of Loretto had reached the end of their options.

Almost twenty years before, four bedraggled nuns had arrived in Santa Fe to answer the call for teachers sent out by Archbishop Jean Baptiste Lamy, who wanted to start an academy for girls in this rather uncivilized western town. The nuns left their home in Bardstown, Kentucky, and embarked on a trip that was difficult and tragic. It took them more than two months to reach their destination. Of the original six nuns who started for Santa Fe, only four arrived. Mother Superior Matilda Mills died en route of cholera on the steamer *Kansas,* and Sister Monica Bailey, who found the trip far too difficult, turned back.

The Academy of Our Lady of Light was the first permanent school for girls in New Mexico Territory. The nuns worked diligently in establishing their school, starting with thirteen students and eventually reaching an enrollment of more than three hundred. Their academy was a success, and many prominent families sent their daughters to be instructed by the Sisters of Loretto, the "Sisters of Our Lady of the Light."

Archbishop Lamy had turned his home, called Casa Americana by the locals, over to the sisters and also loaned them the use of another building that served as the Academy. What the nuns were lacking was a chapel for the Academy.

Construction on the chapel began in 1873, the same year as building commenced on St. Francis Cathedral in Santa Fe. Finally, in 1878, the work was complete. The sisters had dipped heavily into their inheritance to fund this gem, which was a small duplicate of the Sainte-Chapelle in Paris, France, the favorite chapel of Archbishop Lamy during his days in Paris. The original Sainte-Chapelle had been built to please King Louis IX of France.

Their finished chapel soared heavenward, a masterpiece of Gothic majesty. It sat like a princess among its squat, drab neighbors; its sleek, imposing, and adorned lines dominated the adobes of the Santa Fe Trail. Its finished form was a pleasing copy, albeit in miniature, of the prestigious original chapel in Paris.

The builders and the architect were now gone. But what the sisters soon discovered was that the chapel wasn't finished. While the apse, altar, and sanctuary were complete, there was no way to access the choir loft. Whatever means the architect had intended were unknown, for both the architect and his son, who assisted him, were dead.

When Archbishop Lamy had first started construction on St. Francis Cathedral, he discovered that the foundations had been improperly set and thus were dangerous. He sent to France, his homeland, for an architect who was experienced in handling the demands of constructing a majestic Gothic church.

The architect was Antoine Mouly, a Frenchman who was brought to New Mexico to correct the faulty foundations and finish the construction of St. Francis Cathedral. Lamy suggested that while the builders were working on the cathedral, they could also build a small chapel to serve the Sisters of Loretto and their students. The joint construction process would save time and money.

Archbishop Lamy added another qualified French architect, François Mallet, to the Mouly talent pool. Mallet, however, was of little use. He had a roving eye, and it roved to the wife of Lamy's nephew. Jean Baptiste Lamy Jr. warned Mallet to keep away from his wife. When Mallet refused this good advice, Lamy shot him. The younger Lamy was arrested, accused of murder, brought to trial, and acquitted by reason of insanity.

The archbishop assured the architects that they would have no problem finding skilled workmen as there were plenty in the Santa Fe area. The town had a colony of Italian stonemasons who had learned their skills from their immigrant fathers. A number of experienced carpenters were also available. Whatever additional expertise was needed could be acquired from France.

Mouly, who was an old man when he came to America to build the cathedral, was accompanied by his son Projectus. Reportedly, he lost his eyesight while working on the project and was forced to return to France, leaving his son Projectus to finish the work. Projectus, a temperamental fellow, had a stormy relationship with the workers and repeatedly threatened to quit the project.

In 1879 Projectus contracted typhoid fever and died before the chapel was finished, despite all the nursing efforts of the sisters at St. Vincent Hospital. The sensational murder of Mallet and the death of Projectus Mouly added to the lore of the chapel and also contributed to its construction problems. Instead of three qualified architects, the chapel now had none. However, the lack of architects did not impede the building of the cathedral and the chapel. Slowly they rose, marking the flat-roofed adobe skyline of Santa Fe with Gothic classicism.

The Santa Fe community was proud of these two new buildings, and in 1875 the *New Mexican* newspaper reported the progress of the construction:

It was begun somewhat more than a year ago and, since then, work has been continuous by a small force of engineers so that now the rear and sides have attained their full height. In fact, we observe that the first stones for the vaulted roof have been set.

The size of the chapel is 25 feet in width by 75 feet in length including the sanctuary in the middle and the sacristy behind it. It is built in the Gothic style. It is constructed entirely of cut stone using a light brownish sandstone from the Archbishop's quarry east of the city. It has beautifully sculpted pillars and ornament at the door and windows within; two alcoves for statues are also surrounded with artistically embellished sculpted designs while the walls are substantially supported by strong buttresses. All these comprise a substantial degree of perfection, with artistic design as well, which is not exceeded, if equaled, west of the Mississippi valley.

The ceiling is going to be of stone from a porous lava formation, which, with its characteristic lightness, permits this type of roofing and thereby renders the entire structure not only strong in the extreme but absolutely fireproof. The stained glass windows, which were made to order in France with equaled depictions, have already arrived and are ready to be installed when the work is sufficiently advanced.

This detailed description left out a significant lapse in the design: How did one reach the choir loft? The architects were no longer available to provide the answer.

The local company of Monier & Colloudon was hired to finish the cathedral and the chapel. In an 1881 newspaper article, Colloudon's company was recognized as the "builders of . . . the Sisters' new Chapel."

François Guillaume Colloudon originally came from the city of Clermont-Ferrand in France. Archbishop Lamy had attended seminary in Clermont-Ferrand and still had close contacts there who knew of his cathedral and chapel projects.

When Colloudon heard of the money being paid to the workers, he decided in 1874 to come to the United States and seek his fortune in the American West, leaving behind his wife and two children. When he first came over, he traveled around the country for a year. When he reached Colorado, the now disreputable-looking builder threw his bug-infested clothes into the Arkansas River, bought new clothes, and set out on a 230-mile walk to Santa Fe, accompanied only by his donkey.

Colloudon's company drew heavily on the skilled workmen in Santa Fe, including Italian American stonecutters and masons. Records show that Vincente Digneo, Gaetano Palladino, and Luis Moya—men who had Old World skills in the art of stone-masonry—were hired to work on both buildings. The nuns' accounting records also show that local artisans A. Rodriguez and Rafael Martin worked for them.

Unfortunately, the Moulys left behind no design sketches, so without any architectural guidance, the workmen continued on with what had been started. That did not include access to the choir loft. In a letter to his father before his death, Projectus Mouly referred to making "no changes in your prints." However, blueprints for the chapel have not been found in any archives in New Mexico. Perhaps they are hidden in some dusty library in France.

Some have speculated that the original plan was to use a ladder to access the loft. Others thought that an outside staircase was to be constructed. Since the chapel was next to the nuns' school, a few believed that the original design called for a walkway to connect the school's second story to the choir loft, yet no entrance had been built in the wall of either building.

When the nuns first discovered the lack of a staircase, they called in several carpenters. However, the very charm of the chapel, its diminutive size, precluded a standard staircase. The nuns were turned down by builder after builder, who, unfortunately, offered no solution to the dilemma. With no options, no suggestions, and no solutions, the nuns turned their hopeless cause over to a higher authority. They decided to say a novena to St. Joseph, the father of Jesus, a master woodworker, and the patron saint of carpenters.

For nine days the sisters prayed. At the end of the ninth day, a man with a long white beard arrived at the sisters' doorstep, leading a donkey. He had nothing with him but the animal and a toolbox. He asked if they had any work for him. Convinced that their prayers had been answered, they showed him the chapel and explained their need for a staircase to the choir loft.

The carpenter set to work immediately, only asking the nuns to supply him with two large tubs of water. One of the sisters remembered entering the chapel and seeing wood soaking in the tubs.

It took eight months for the carpenter to finish the staircase. When the nuns viewed the finished product, they were stunned by its simplicity and the ingenuity of the staircase design. Located off to the left side of the chapel, with one end leading to the choir loft and the other firmly planted on the chapel's floor, was a wooden staircase twisting and turning upon itself, rising the twenty-plus feet to the loft. It was a masterpiece of two 360-degree turns described as a double helix. Adding to its mysticism, it showed no visible means of support. Its construction was unique: It was made entirely of wood and was held together with wooden dowels and pegs. The nuns were ecstatic. Not only did they have their staircase, but it was a thing of beauty.

Courtesy Palace of the Governors Photo Archives (NMHM/DCA), #HP.2007.20.88

The "Miraculous Staircase" at Loretto Chapel,
Santa Fe, New Mexico.

When they went to express their gratitude to the carpenter and settle up the account, he had disappeared. They searched for their mysterious carpenter, but no one knew who he was, where he came from, or where he went. That is when they concluded that it must have been St. Joseph himself who answered their prayers and built their staircase.

Even the staircase was a mystery. The wood used in the staircase was unique, for it was not local wood and its origin could not be identified. Moreover, the staircase had no visible means of support. Surely these strange elements about the staircase proved that it was divine intervention, not man's creative ability, that had given the nuns their staircase.

However, some people have offered less spiritual answers to the mystery of this beautiful staircase. Over the years, several mortal craftsmen have been identified as the builder of the staircase.

The most popular candidate is François-Jean Rochas, a member of "les compagnons," a secretive French guild of craftsmen. He supposedly showed up one day with a burro laden with carpentry tools. In an article that appeared in the *New Mexican* newspaper in 1895, Quinitus Monier identified Rochas as the builder of the staircase. The sisters' daybook also has a notation that a Mr. Rochas received $150 for wood, giving some credence to this identification. A freight slip has been found stating that wood was delivered by ship from France and might even have been brought over by Rochas himself.

In reality, the chances that Rochas would appear suddenly to work on a small chapel (with his own wood) and never build anything else in Santa Fe, before or after, is hard to believe. The only other construction project attributed to Rochas is the stone walls surrounding his property.

The character of this reclusive hermit, who was far from being a saintly man, also makes it doubtful that he would anonymously attend to good deeds. Rochas met his death mysteriously through either suicide or murder in his Dog Canyon hideaway. Curiously, after his death, three letters mentioning Archbishop Lamy were found in Rochas's cabin.

Another candidate for the role of the builder of the stairs was Don Jose Antonio Rodriguez, a man plagued by his wayward son. Rodriguez turned toward God and made a covenant that if his son reformed, he would perform a service to the Church. Reportedly, he worked early in the morning so as not to interfere with the nuns' prayers. He also swore Mother Superior Magdalen Hayden to secrecy. He wanted no one to learn of his son's unacceptable behavior.

According to legend, Rodriguez received no pay for his work, but nuns' accounting notes between 1875 and 1876 do show a recurring payment made to A. Rodriguez for work on a "two-story house," which could have been Casa Americana, the nun's home. Did he also build the chapel staircase? The Rodriguez family thought so. Mary Rodriguez was always told that her grandfather, Don Jose Antonio Rodriguez, was the builder of the chapel's spiral staircase.

The Rodriguezes are not the only family to claim that their ancestor had constructed the famous staircase. In a newspaper article written in 1970, Oscar Hadwiger claimed that his grandfather, Yohon L. Hadwiger from Vienna, Austria, was the mastermind behind the stairs. Hadwiger came to America in 1877, looking for his young son John, who had run off to the New World. He found his son, but John did not want to return to Austria. Not willing to waste the trip, Yohon decided to tour the West and headed for Colorado. He heard about the silver and gold strikes and thought he would try his hand at prospecting. When he returned to Austria, he wrote his son that he had built some stairs in a Santa Fe church but hadn't completed them. To support his claim, the grandson produced a rough sketch made by Yohon in 1878 of a double-helix design.

This claim infuriated the Sisters of Loretto, who insisted that Hadwiger refrain from making this claim. The mother superior wrote: "It is just an imaginary statement on your part that the man who built the Stairs was your Grandfather—a fine builder of Stairs—but to make a definite statement without proof it was your Grandfather would be an evasion of the truth since Mother Magdalen herself wrote to the Mother Superior making the statement that she did not know the man just a short time after he disappeared. Even if you had proof we could not accept it since there is not a Sister living today who could identify him."

It is quite possible that the staircase was actually built in France and shipped to Santa Fe, where it was installed by a local carpenter. That carpenter could be any one of the men who claimed that they had actually built the stairs. It is not unknown for someone to take credit for another's work, especially in the Old West, where records were scanty and the art of embellishing the truth was a way of life.

Some have wondered at the staircase's lack of any visible means of support. However, the staircase actually does have some structural support. First, a metal support bracket at the top of the stairs attaches to one of the chapel's pillars. Second, the double-helix design itself provides support. The spiral outside structures holding the stairs turn in such a small radius that the inner stringer functions as a solid pole. Nonetheless, the passage of time has weakened the staircase. In its present wobbly state, the staircase has been closed off.

The type of wood used in the staircase has also presented a conundrum. Until a few years ago, no one could identify it. Recently, though, a small sample of the wood was given to the U.S. Forest Service's Center for Wood Anatomy Research for analysis. This organization has identified some interesting wood, including the ladder used in the Lindbergh kidnapping and artifacts from King Tut's tomb.

The research center found that the chapel wood belonged to the spruce family and described it as "a type of light, strong, elastic wood" used in construction. This species of wood can be found around the world, including America. However, no trees of this type have been found in the Santa Fe area.

Answers have been proposed to all the mysteries surrounding the stairs, but are these answers correct? The exact identity of the builder of the chapel stairs is not yet known with certainty. Nor can the origin of the wood be pinpointed with any accuracy.

While slightly unstable, the staircase still stands. But then it was built sometime between 1877 and 1881. Any structure that old deserves to be somewhat rickety.

Over the years, a Gothic altar, frescos, and the Stations of the Cross were added, lending a holy and peaceful atmosphere to the diminutive chapel.

The Academy of Our Lady of Light, which adjoined the sisters' chapel, was closed in 1968. At that time, the chapel was deconsecrated. But nothing has diminished either the chapel's beauty or the wonder of the staircase. This inspiring and graceful Gothic chapel, with its unique and inexplicable staircase, is now a private museum open to the public. Whether a mortal or a saint built the staircase hardly matters. It truly is a heavenly work of art and an inspired piece of engineering.

CHAPTER THIRTEEN

Lincoln: The Town of Legends

The main street in Lincoln is about a mile long. But in the nineteenth century, step for step, it held more aggravation and lawlessness than any other measured mile in New Mexico. Down its hard-packed dirt road walked the boots of such legends as Billy the Kid, politician Thomas B. Catron, cattle baron John Chisum, rustler Jesse Evans, and many other men of questionable reputation.

Lincoln got its start peacefully enough in 1849 when Spanish pioneers settled the area, attracted by the proximity of the River Bonito and the lushness of the land, which promised good farming. They aptly named their settlement La Placita del Rio Bonito (Village by the Pretty River). This mouthful was soon shortened to La Placita. Within two years, Mescalero Apaches, who claimed the territory as their own, violently shattered the peaceful lifestyle of this village.

In 1855 the army established Fort Stanton a few miles away from La Placita to protect the pioneers who were moving into the area and to oversee the Mescalero Indian reservation. With the establishment of Fort Stanton, the village finally had some relief from the Apache raids.

Whatever peace was achieved was not long-lasting. With the fort and the Indian reservation came demands for beef and supplies, a situation that invited corruption and crime.

In 1869 Lawrence G. Murphy, the post trader at nearby Fort Stanton, encouraged Captain Saturnino Baca to sponsor a bill that would create a new county. Baca named the new county Lincoln, and the village of La Placita, the largest town in the new county, was renamed Lincoln. Murphy, his future partner James Dolan, and Major William Brady, all from the fort, would have a huge impact on the new direction of Lincoln and would leave fingerprints of violence on the town.

Four years after Lincoln became a new county, the drama started. Murphy and Dolan were charged with suspicious business practices in dealing with supplies sold to the army and the Indians, and they were ordered to leave Fort Stanton. They set up their trading business in the town of Lincoln. The clever Murphy never overlooked an opportunity to better his situation, and he and Dolan aligned themselves with the Santa Fe Ring, the corrupt political cabal that ran the New Mexico Territory. One of its most active members was Thomas B. Catron, who was New Mexico's U.S. district attorney. The Murphy Company was especially friendly with Catron and gladly financed several loans when he needed money. In less than twenty-five years from its founding, this village by the pretty river went from a peaceful settlement to a hotbed of corruption.

Murphy built a two-story store and from there supplied beef and flour to Fort Stanton and the nearby Mescalero Apache reservation. But old business practices die hard, especially profitable ones. It wasn't long before there were whispers about Murphy and his partners concerning cheating and dishonest practices.

The beef contracts were highly profitable, and beef was hard to find. Murphy's store solved that dilemma by hiring Jesse Evans and his rustling friends to supply the needed beef, thus ensuring a huge profit for Murphy and his partners.

Evans was well suited for his new employment. He was half Cherokee, and this probably gave him the instincts for survival that served him well in his life. For an outlaw, he was unique, having graduated from Washington and Lee College in Virginia. But something went wrong. Instead of leading an exemplary life, Evans became one of the West's cruelest and most feared outlaws. Even Billy the Kid was afraid of Evans.

Evans worked for a while as a cowboy for John Chisum. After leaving Chisum, he wandered around New Mexico and then joined the notorious John Kinney Gang. In the evening of December 31, 1875, the Kinney Gang, including Evans, rode into Las Cruces and became involved in a brawl with soldiers stationed at Fort Seldon. The soldiers won the fight, and the outlaws turned tail. Later, however, they returned and shot up the saloon, killing two soldiers and one civilian.

Feeling confident after that shootout, Evans started his own gang. Known throughout the territory as the Jesse Evans Gang, they coined the name "The Boys" for themselves. The Boys spent their time robbing and cattle rustling in Lincoln County. Their reputation as fearsome rustlers grew, and in 1877 they were hired by the Murphy faction. Their job was to supply the beef Murphy needed to fill his government contracts, as well as to do any odd jobs Murphy required. It was one of these odd jobs that cemented Evans's outlaw reputation and kicked off the Lincoln County War.

In 1877 competition for Murphy and Dolan came to town in the persons of Alexander A. McSween and John H. Tunstall. Tunstall's father was a wealthy merchant in London, England; McSween was a midwestern lawyer with high principles and ideals. They joined forces to fight the unscrupulous reign of the Murphy Company.

Tunstall and McSween formed a partnership and built a mercantile store on the other side of the street from the Murphy-Dolan establishment. They went after government contracts, offering the first competition Murphy and Dolan had experienced. The people in and around Lincoln, who were weary of the unfair prices and heavy-handed business practices of Murphy and Dolan, welcomed the competition. In partnership with John S. Chisum, the famous rancher, Tunstall also established the Lincoln County Bank.

Pushed to the wall by these Tunstall enterprises, the Murphy faction turned to underhanded manipulations and accusations that ended with a five-day shootout called the Lincoln County War. This confrontation was based not on cattle or a fight for land, but on a battle for government contracts—an economic war.

What kicked off the war was a diabolical scheme by Murphy. He had Tunstall's cattle attached on trumped-up charges. The cattle and Tunstall's horses were at Tunstall's ranch. When Tunstall tried to remove them, Sheriff William Brady and his deputies threatened him and his men with legal action and violence. Wanting to find a peaceful means to solve his situation, Tunstall decided to leave the cattle at the ranch with Murphy's man, Sheriff Brady, until the matter was settled in the courts. His horses, however, were not under the attachment, and he decided to take them back to Lincoln.

On the morning of February 18, 1878, Tunstall—accompanied by his ranch foreman, John Brewer; Robert Widenmann; John Middleton; and Billy the Kid—set out for Lincoln. Along the trail, they spotted some wild turkeys, and Tunstall encouraged his men to hunt them while he waited with the horses. Riding to the top of the ridge, the hunting party heard hoofbeats below. They turned to see a group of men bearing down on Tunstall. By the time Tunstall's men reached him, he had been shot and killed. Widenmann recognized Evans among the disappearing killers. However, Tunstall's friends were outnumbered five to one, and pursuit would have been dangerous.

Since none of Tunstall's men had actually witnessed the killing, nothing could be done legally to arrest and charge the suspects. Evans had done his job well. He had eliminated part of Murphy and Dolan's competition, but in doing so he had ignited the tinder that blazed up into the Lincoln County War.

The Tunstall and McSween faction, known as the Regulators, set about avenging Tunstall's death. On March 9, Tunstall and McSween supporters formed a vigilante posse and caught and killed William Morton and Frank Baker, two of Murphy's men. They managed to shoot Evans as he was escaping. The wounded Evans was found and arrested, but he escaped from jail and eventually returned to Lincoln to fight in the war.

County court in Lincoln was scheduled for April 8, 1878, but somehow word got out that the session was on April 1. Six Regulators, including Billy the Kid, arrived in town the night before and stayed at Tunstall's store. Some were the accused, and some were witnesses, and they wanted to be on hand early for the court session.

About 9:00 a.m. on April 1, Sheriff Brady, with his deputies George Hindman, Jacob Mathews, John Long, and George Peppin, left Dolan's store. Their walk to the courthouse took them past Tunstall's store. Several prospective jurors were waiting outside the courthouse, and the sheriff informed them of the mix-up in court dates and asked them to return on April 8. Having done their official duty, the men wandered back toward the Murphy-Dolan store in separate small groups. As Sheriff Brady and Hindman walked past Tunstall's store, shots rang out from the adobe wall bordering the store's driveway. Brady dropped, mortally wounded. Hindman, also wounded, staggered backwards toward the Montano store and fell. Ike Stockton, who ran a saloon in the corner of the store, came running out in time to hear Hindman calling for water. Stockton ran to the creek, but when he returned with the water, Hindman was dead.

Billy the Kid and some of the Regulators rushed out from behind the wall. Billy stopped to pick up a rifle Brady had taken from him earlier and was immediately shot by one of Murphy's supporters. The shot went through Billy's left thigh, forcing him to hide in town for several days until he could sit a horse. Lincoln resident Sam Corbett took in the wounded Billy. When the soldiers from Fort Stanton came looking for the Kid, Corbett stashed him in a hole under his bed, where Billy hid with a gun ready in his hand.

There were several Regulators on the Tunstall property that morning, so it was impossible to tell who had fired the shots that had killed Brady and Hindman. Nonetheless, Billy the Kid was blamed without proof. Eventually the soldiers gave up looking, and Billy safely rode out of Lincoln.

Not wanting anything to do with the feud between the Regulators and the Murphy group, Ike Stockton left Lincoln soon after that gunfight. However, he turned out to be less than a good citizen. Ike and his brother Porter started their own gang. They relocated in the area around Farmington, New Mexico, and Durango, Colorado, where they spent their days and nights robbing trains and rustling cattle. The law caught up with Porter at his ranch, and he died in the ensuing gun battle.

Ike, hearing of his brother's death, went on a killing rampage, and in a gun battle with the law in Durango, he was shot in the left knee. Trying to save his life, the town doctor amputated Ike's leg, but Stockton was dead within a few hours. And so, two more of Lincoln's residents were destined for infamy.

To avenge the killing of Brady and Hindman, Evans and his men retaliated by killing one Regulator, Frank McNab, and wounding another, Ab Saunders, on April 29, 1878. On April 30, several "friends" of Evans were killed, and the Regulators were suspected. The lines had been drawn, and McSween feared for his life.

The killing reached its climax with a battle that commenced on Sunday, July 14, when about fifty of McSween's supporters rode into Lincoln. They distributed themselves around town. The largest group, twenty-five Mexicans under the command of Martin Chavez, settled at the Montano store. Some went to the Ellis house to guard the eastern end of town. Billy the Kid, his friend Tom O'Folliard, and about a dozen other gunmen were stationed at McSween's house.

The McSween protectors caught Sheriff Peppin shorthanded. He had sent most of his men to the village of San Patricio, believing that the McSween force would rendezvous there. A message was sent to the posse recalling them to Lincoln.

The McSween men set about fortifying their buildings. They barricaded the windows, placed bags of dirt by the doorways, and drilled holes for shooting. They were ready for a siege.

Peppin's posse arrived in Lincoln late in the afternoon. Among the riders were Wallace Olinger, whose brother Robert would later be killed by Billy the Kid, and Jesse Evans. The manpower of both sides was now about even. Most of the residents had left town, and the few who remained kept to their homes. Once the Murphy men were strategically deployed, the battle commenced. A spate of heavy firing started late in the afternoon of July 15. The casualty toll on the first day was light. Only a mule and a horse were killed.

The next day the shooting was intermittent as each side tried to solidify its positions. That day ended with no casualties. Peppin tried to get Colonel N. A. M. Dudley from Fort Stanton to intervene, but Dudley was under orders not to interfere with civilian disputes.

Wednesday, July 17, started out quietly. The men Peppin had stationed up on the hillsides saw no activity around McSween's house, and so they decided to head back to their headquarters at the Wortley Hotel. Feeling secure, they took no precautions as they headed down the hills into town. They became perfect targets for McSween's men in the Montano house.

The Regulators' best shot, Fernando Herrera, hit Charlie Crawford, wounding him so severely that he couldn't even crawl to safety. Not a single Peppin man was willing to try a rescue, and Crawford lay in the hot sun all morning.

That afternoon several officers arrived from Fort Stanton. They were there to investigate the shooting of Berry Robinson, one of their soldiers who had accidentally gotten in the line of fire a few days earlier. First they interviewed the Murphy men at the Wortley Hotel. Then they walked over to McSween's house to further investigate the incident. Of course, the two stories were significantly different. But because the officers were partial to Murphy's men, they ruled that McSween's men had deliberately fired on the soldier.

Dr. D. M. Appel took this lull in the gun battle to tend to Crawford, who was still lying on the hillside where he had been shot. His hip wound was serious, and he was suffering from exposure. Dr. Appel was able to transport him to the hospital at Fort Stanton, but Crawford died five weeks later from his wounds.

Thursday, July 18, again started out quietly. Rumors were more active than guns as the talk was first that McSween was procuring a 16-pounder gun and then that Peppin was attempting to acquire a howitzer. Neither rumor proved true. Meanwhile, Colonel Dudley at Fort Stanton was still vacillating on whether he should intervene in the Lincoln battle.

Friday, the fifth day of the conflict, started with a bang. The exchange of shots began at 7:00 a.m. During the night Murphy's men had gathered at the Wortley Hotel. They were ready to surround McSween's house and end the struggle by any means, fair or foul.

Finally, Colonel Dudley made up his mind. With an attachment of thirty-five men and all but one of Fort Stanton's officers, he headed for Lincoln. They set up their campsite in a vacant lot between two of the places held by McSween's men. Dudley ordered McSween's men at the Ellis and the Montano houses to evacuate the premises and to cease their gunfighting. These two groups made up about two-thirds of the McSween fighting men. The men mounted their horses and left town, leaving the McSween faction seriously undergunned.

As the soldiers moved up and down the street, Murphy's men joined them and were able to get closer to McSween's house. McSween's men could not fire for fear of hitting the soldiers.

Several of Murphy's men were able to get close enough to the McSween house to start two fires. Mrs. Shield, McSween's sister-in-law, extinguished one of the fires by pouring all their available water over it, leaving them nothing to fight the other fire. The second fire slowly made its way through the building. Under cover of darkness Mrs. McSween, her sister Mrs. Shield, and the children escaped from the house. The fire had now reached the last room in the house.

At nightfall Billy the Kid and several others made their move. The plan was for them to depart the house and exit from the east side, drawing attention away from McSween,

FRASHER, COURTESY PALACE OF THE GOVERNORS PHOTO ARCHIVES (NMHM/DCA), #105473

The main street in Lincoln, New Mexico, circa 1879, site of the burned McSween house and Tunstall store.

who would leave from the north side of the house. What happened then is a story of confusion and conjecture. Some say that McSween's men offered to surrender but changed their minds and shot at the approaching Murphy men. Others say that one of the Murphy men drew a bead on McSween and that another Murphy man, Bob Beckwith, shoved the gun aside. The unfortunate result was that Beckwith was hit by the bullet and died. Whatever the exact details, McSween was shot and killed leaving his house. The Lincoln County War was over.

Billy the Kid escaped that night. Although his days as a free man were numbered, he was not through contributing to the legends of Lincoln. The Kid was captured by Pat Garrett, indicted for the murder of Sheriff Brady, and found guilty.

He was brought to Lincoln, where County Sheriff Pat Garrett locked him up in a room in the northeast corner of the second floor of the courthouse. The courthouse, which had formerly been the Murphy-Dolan store, was owned by Thomas Catron, who acquired it after the Lincoln County War and generously gave it (or sold it) to Lincoln County for its courthouse.

Billy was guarded by deputies Robert Olinger and J. W. Bell. Olinger in particular had a hatred for Billy and delighted in taunting him. Somehow Billy obtained a gun. The most logical explanation is that a sympathetic young Lincoln man by the name of Jose M. Aguayo hid a gun in the town outhouse, which was used by civilians and prisoners. When Bell saw Billy with a gun, he tried to sound a warning, but Billy killed him inside the building. Billy then shot Olinger, who was outside, from the balcony. Billy was able to escape, only to be hunted and gunned down by Pat Garrett at the Maxwell Ranch.

Jesse Evans fared a little better. After the Lincoln County War, he continued his life of crime but was eventually captured by the Texas Rangers, brought to trial, and convicted of murdering Tunstall. He was sentenced to ten years in the state prison at Huntsville, Texas. After two years he escaped and disappeared.

All good legends have a twist, and so it is with this one. In 1948 Joe Hines, an elderly man in Florida, claimed the land of his recently deceased brother in Missouri, stating he was the brother of the deceased. That meant that Hines was Jesse Evans. Joe Hines convinced the Missouri investigator and was awarded the land. Joe Hines also insisted that Billy the Kid did not die at the Maxwell Ranch but escaped to Hico, Texas, where he lived as Ollie P. Roberts. Thomas Catron, who was also connected to the Lincoln County War, wound up in Washington, D.C., as New Mexico's first U.S. senator.

When you walk the main street in Lincoln, be careful where you tread. You are stepping in the footfalls of some famous legends.

BIBLIOGRAPHY

The Lost Adams Gold

Dobie, J. Frank. *Apache Gold and Yaqui Silver.* Austin: University of Texas Press, 1939.

French, Richard. *Four Days from Fort Wingate: The Lost Adams Diggings.* Caldwell, ID: Caxton Printers, 1994.

Harden, Paul. "The Lost Adams Diggings." Socorro, NM: *El Defensor Chieftain,* September 4, 2004.

Purcell, Jack. *The Lost Adams Diggings: Myth, Mystery, and Madness.* Olathe, KS: NineLives Press.

http://en.wikipedia.org/wiki/Fort_Wingate

http://en.wikipedia.org/wiki/Lost_Adams_Diggings

http://hubpages.com/hub/The-Lost-Adams-Diggings

www.goldfeverprospecting.com/loaddipa1.html

www.lostadams.com/GPAA%20Story%201%20Page%201.jpg

www.thegeozone.com/treasure/new_mexico/tales/nm002a.jsp

The Disappearance of a People

Frazier, Kendrick. *People of Chaco: A Canyon and Its Culture.* New York: W.W. Norton, 1986.

Lekson, Stephen H. "The Center of the Universe." *Discovering Archaeology,* May–June 1990.

Lourie, Peter. *The Lost World of the Anasazi.* Honesdale, PA: Boyds Mills Press, 2007.

La Llorona: The Weeping Woman

Beatty, Judith S., and Edward Garcia Kraul, eds. *La Llorona: Encounters with the Weeping Woman.* Santa Fe, NM: Sunstone Press, 2004.

Lowery, Linda, and Richard Keep. *The Tale of La Llorona.* Minneapolis: Lerner Publishing, 2008.

www.legendsofamerica.com/HC-AlbuquerqueGhosts.html

www.legendsofamerica.com/HC-WeepingWoman1.html

Who Killed the Colonel and Little Henry?

Bullis, Don, ed. "Hillsboro: Boomtown to Ghost Town." *The New Mexico Historical Notebook* 2, no. 20 (March 1, 2006): 6–7.

Fulton, Maurice G. *History of the Lincoln County War: A Classic Account of Billy the Kid.* Tucson: University of Arizona Press, 1968.

Recko, Corey. "Pinkerton Operative John C. Frazer." *Journal of Wild West History* 1, no. 2 (April 2008): 5–18.

———. *Murder on the White Sands: The Disappearance of Albert and Henry Fountain*. Denton: University of North Texas Press, 2007.

The Secret of the School on the Hill

Hunner, Jon. *Inventing Los Alamos: The Growth of an Atomic Community*. Norman: University of Oklahoma Press, 2004.

Los Alamos: Beginning of an Era, 1943–1945. LASL Public Relations Office.

Szasz, Ferenc M., and George E. Webb. "The New Mexico Response to the End of the Second World War." *New Mexico Historical Review* 83, no. 1 (Winter 2008).

Trinity Site, 1945–1995. Washington, DC: Government Printing Office.

www.wsmr.army.mil/wsmr.asp?pg=y&pge+587

The Curious Cowboy and the Mysterious Bones

Folsom, Franklin. *The Life and Legend of George McJunkin: Black Cowboy*. Nashville: Thomas Nelson, 1973.

http://en.wikipedia.org/wiki/Clovis_culture

http://findarticles.com/p/articles/mi_m1134/is_nl_v106/ai_19318723/

http://smu.edu/anthro/QUEST/Projects/Folsom.htm

www.co.colfax.nm.us/history.htm

www.cyberwest.com/cw03/v3adwst2.html

www.folsomvillage.com/folsommuseum/georgemcjunkin.html

www.sangres.com/history/firstamericans/htm

The Treasure of Victorio Peak

Jameson, W. C. *New Mexico Treasure Tales.* Caldwell, ID: Caxton Press, 2003.

Schweidel, David, and Robert Boswell. *What Men Call Treasure: The Search for Gold at Victorio Peak.* El Paso, TX: Cinco Puntos Press, 2008.

http://farshores.org/a03smvp.htm

www.legendsofamerica.com/HC-Treasures5.html

www.mcguiresplace.net/The%20Treasure%of%20 Victorio%20Peak

www.theoutlaws.com/gold7.htm

The Crash That Never Happened

Carey, Thomas. Personal communication, March 30, 2010.

Carey, Thomas, and Donald R. Schmitt. *Witness to Roswell: Unmasking the Government's Biggest Cover-Up.* Franklin Lakes, NJ: New Page Books, 2009.

Korff, Kal K. *The Roswell UFO Crash: What They Don't Want You to Know.* New York: Dell, 1997.

Marcel, Jesse, Jr., and Linda Marcel. *The Roswell Legacy: The Untold Story of the First Military Officer at the 1947 Crash Site.* Franklin Lakes, NJ: New Page Books, 2009.

Pflock, Karl T. *Roswell: Inconvenient Facts and the Will to Believe.* Amherst, NY: Prometheus Books, 2001.

http://en.wikipedia.org/wiki/Glenn_Dennis

http://en.wikipedia.org/wiki/Roswell_UFO_Incident

www.archives.gov/foia/ufos.html

www.legendsofamerica.com/NM-RoswellUFO.html

www.roswellproof.com/dennis.html

www.roswellufomuseum.com/incident1.htm

The Madness of the Mayberry Murders

Rasch, Phillip J. "New Mexico's Most Ruthless Murder." *True West,* November–December 1971.

White, James W. *The History of Lincoln County Post Offices.* Farmington, NM: James W. White, 2007.

http://newmexicoalhn.net/fhmurder_bonita.htm

http://hollowhill.com/bonito-city-the-real-story

www.ghosttowns.com/states/nm/bonitocity.html

www.livestockweekly.com/papers/96/10/03/3bonitolake.asp

www.stacyhorn.com/unbelievable/?p=1344

The Half Man

Meldrum, Jeff. *Sasquatch: Legend Meets Science.* New York: Tom Doherty Associates, 2006.

http://en.wikipedia.org/wiki/Bigfoot

http://en.wikiedia.org/wiki/Evidence_regarding_Bigfoot

http://mystrangenewmexico.com

www.bfro.net/GDB/CNTS/CA/DN/ca_dm004/htm

www.bfro.net/GDB/show_article.asp?id=568

www.bfro.net/GDB/show_county_reports.asp?stte=nm& county=Otero

www.bfro.net/GDB/state_listing.asp?stte=NM

www.bfro.net/news/roundup/expNM2004_report.asp

www.epodunk.com/cgi-gin/genInfo.php?locIndex=17916

www.livescience.com/strangenews/071203-yeti-reports.html

A Ghostly Assortment of Dubious Characters

Hart, Herbert M. *Old Forts of the Southwest.* New York: Bonanza Books, 1986.

Jameson, W. C. *Legend and Lore of the Guadalupe Mountains.* Albuquerque: University of New Mexico Press, 2007.

Kermeen, Frances. *Ghostly Encounters: True Stories of America's Haunted Inns and Hotels.* New York: Warner Books, 2002.

http://en.wikipedia.org/wiki/Fort_Union_National Monument

www.city-data.com/city/Nageezi-New-Mexico.html

www.epodunk.com/cgi-bin/genInfo.php?locIndex=17912

www.ghostsofamerica.com/8/NewMexicoNageezighostsightings.html

www.hauntedhouses.com/states/nm/saint_james_hotel.cfm

www.legendsofamerica.come/Ah-DeathWaltz.html

www.legendsofamerica.com/nm-cimarron.html

www.legendsofamerica.com/nm-stjameshotel.html

www.newmexico.org/western/experience/st_james.php

www.nps.gov/srchive/foun/adhi/adhi1.htm

The Stairs from Heaven

Bullock, Alice. *Loretto and the Miraculous Staircase.* Santa Fe, NM: Sunstone Press, 1978.

Straw, Mary J. *Loretto: The Sisters and Their Santa Fe Chapel.* Santa Fe, NM: West America Publishing, 1884.

http://culbreath.wordpress.com/2007/10/19/loretto-chapels-miraculous-staircase/

www.csicop.org/si/9811/i-files.html

www.lorettochapel.com/history.html

Lincoln: The Town of Legends

"The Escape of 'The Kid!'" *The New Southwest and Herald,* Silver City, NM, May 14, 1881, in *Western Outlaw–Lawman History Association Journal,* Winter 2007.

Fulton, Maurice G. *History of the Lincoln County War: A Classic Account of Billy the Kid.* Tucson: University of Arizona Press, 1997.

Kadlec, Robert F. *They Knew Billy the Kid.* Santa Fe, NM: Ancient City Press, 1987.

O'Neal, Bill. *Encyclopedia of Western Gunfighters.* Norman: University of Oklahoma Press, 1979.

http://en.wikipedia.org/wiki/Jessie_evans_(outlaw)

http://en.wikipedia.org/wiki/Jessie_Evans_Gang

http://en.wikipedia.org/wiki/Lincoln_County_War

www.aboutbillythekid.com/Lincoln_County_War.htm

www.globalsecurity.org/military/ops/lincoln-county-war.htm

www.newmexico.org/billthekid/billypages/Lincoln_county_war
.php

www.southernnewmexico.com/Articles/Southeast/Lincoln/
TheLincolnCountyWar.html

www.spartacus.schoolnet.co.uk/WWlincolnwar.htm

INDEX

ABOUT THE AUTHOR

Barbara Marriott has a PhD in cultural anthropology, a thirst for knowledge, and an insatiable curiosity, giving her the enthusiasm and the tools to research, analyze, and weave together people, cultures, and events. Barbara is the author of several books on the Old West, including *Outlaw Tales of New Mexico* (TwoDot), *Annie's Guests,* and *Canyon of Gold.* She lives in Tucson, Arizona.